Advance praise fo so
by Danai Chanchaochai

"If the Buddha gave advice in a newspaper column today, he might sound like this book's author. . . . His is a unique perspective, blending Western-style corporate considerations with the outlook of an Asian culture seasoned by a long history of Buddhist thought and practice. Much has been written on Buddhism and meditation, but the application of Buddism to the workplace is less familiar and a welcome extension of morality and ethics to daily life. . . . Anyone interested in practical, everyday dharma for beginners can find a lesson in this book."

Publishers Weekly

"We all have 'Dharma moments' in our lives—times when our choices can make or break our journey. This beautiful book lovingly uses the teachings of Buddha to guide us through the darker corridors of our lives."

Dr. Stephen R. Covey, author, *The 7 Habits of Highly Effective People* and *The 8th Habit: From Effectiveness to Greatness*

"It is indeed heartening to see how even people caught up in the swirl of business and modern city life can apply this age-old wisdom imparted by the Buddha. It is like taking a cool shower on a sultry day."

Professor Richard Gombrich, Boden Professor of Sanskrit Emeritus, Oxford University

Academic Director, Oxford Centre for Buddhist Studies

Dharma Moments

Dharma Moments

Danai Chanchaochai

NICHOLAS BREALEY
PUBLISHING

BOSTON • LONDON

This edition first published by Nicholas Brealey Publishing in 2006.

100 City Hall Plaza, Suite 501
Boston, MA 02108 USA
Tel: 617-523-3801
Fax: 617-523-3708
www.nicholasbrealey.com

3-5 Spafield Street, Clerkenwell
London, EC1R 4QB, UK
Tel: +44-(0)-207-239-0360
Fax: +44-(0)-207-239-0370
www.nbrealey-books.com

Editor: Kelvin Rugg

Printed in the United States of America
10 09 08 07 06   1 2 3 4 5

ISBN-13: 978-1-85788-385-5
ISBN-10: 1-85788-385-3

Library of Congress Cataloging-in-Publication Data
Danai Chanchaochai.
Dharma moments / Danai Chanchaochai.
p. cm.
ISBN-13: 978-1-85788-385-5
ISBN-10: 1-85788-385-3
1. Religious life--Buddhism. 2. Interpersonal relations--Religious
aspects--Buddhism.
I. Title.
BQ5395.D36 2006

294.3'442--dc22
2005023559

THE DALAI LAMA

Introduction

Shakyamuni Buddha attained enlightenment and taught in India over two thousand and five hundred years ago, yet his teaching remains refreshing and relevant today. No matter who we are or where we live, we all want happiness and dislike suffering. The Buddha counseled, therefore, that we should help others as much as we can and even if we cannot actually be of help, we should at least not do anyone harm.

Part of Buddhist practice involves training our minds through meditation. But if our training in calming our minds, developing qualities like love, compassion, generosity and patience, is to be effective, we must put them into practice in day-to-day life. This book *Dharma Moments* contains plentiful contemporary advice on how we can do that in words that are easy to understand. The Buddha's teachings are both subtle and profound, but it is very important that they are made accessible in a way that people can actually put them into effect and derive real benefit from them. I am sure this book will achieve this and that it will prove helpful to general readers, especially those who have little previous acquaintance with Buddhism, as well as dedicated Buddhists who have little time to read and study more widely, but are looking for something to inspire them here and now.

Contents

Foreword by Prapai Kraisornkovit

FOREWORD

Danai Chanchaochai started his weekly column, "Dharma Moments," in the *Bangkok Post's* Real.Time section in August 2002. In it he explores everyday social karma with a keen insight in our civil microcosm—a simple guide that advocates a different approach. His writing provides a refreshing perception that makes us pause and think what and who we are in the social labyrinth of society.

In the chaos of modern city life, we assume others should practice the common courtesies that we ourselves often overlook. We rush though our daily routine with such frightening monotony that we tend to fall victim to our own bad habits without realizing it. We make snap judgments of others, carelessly ignoring our own karma. Our moral actions greatly affect our lives and the lives of others.

Everyone can benefit from a little clarity. Many people search for focus through meditation, eager to retune senses dulled with images of happiness, success, and riches from countless television and radio images. Our perceptions have become obscured and tainted with each new advertising campaign. We frequently forget that the path to self-realization and ultimate peace lies within us.

Dharma Moments provides a tangible reference to a "betterself." The dialogues are realistic scenarios to which everyone can relate. The lessons learned are easy to understand. The advice is gentle. The passages are concise and elegant.

This book is a compilation of Danai's perceptions translated into subtly worded articles, in which he makes many delightful observations. Danai uses simple approaches to put forward key ideas, be they personal such as self-image, social as in common courtesy or the psyche of first impressions. His insights into social customs and morals are truly inspirational. His gentle style stimulates our consciousness and stirs quiet moments of reflection.

It is hard to get good and free advice nowadays. Friends are sometimes biased out of loyalty. Parents don't always understand the problems. *Dharma Moments* offers sound, non-biased advice for people of all ages and for all occasions.

Prapai Kraisornkovit
Editor, Real.Time
Bangkok Post

Dharma teachings

The great awakening

The Lord Buddha's teachings help us to
create a sense of perspective

One of the many stories about
the Buddha tells of how, soon after his Enlightenment he
happened upon a man along the road who was struck by
the Buddha's extraordinary radiance and peaceful presence.
The man stopped and asked, "My friend, what are you? Are
you a celestial being or a god?"

"I am neither," said the Buddha.

"Well, then, are you a magician or a wizard?"

"No," replied the Buddha.

"Then what are you?"

"I am awake," said the Buddha.

Can we say the same thing about ourselves? Are we truly awake, really mindful of the world in which we live, fully aware of all its temptations on the one hand and the enormous potential for good it offers on the other?

Being unaware of even the physical world around us seems to be an increasing phenomenon in what is today's consumer-oriented world. We often tend to encounter people so wrapped up with their own affairs that they will, for instance, pause to hold a family conversation at the foot of a busy escalator or stop to window-shop on a narrow pavement, apparently unconcerned or unaware that others are being inconvenienced by their actions.

Certainly, they cannot claim to be awake. That type of unawareness may seem trivial, the action of individuals so preoccupied with their own affairs that they are unmindful of their surroundings or the presence of other people. It is however, symptomatic of a situation in which we can all find ourselves when we lose sight of the need to be mindful of every moment.

This of course is where the Buddha's teachings can be so helpful. They offer sound practical advice on staying aware of the world in which we live, of being awake.

Let's look at some of the ways this advice can help to change our lives, to give them the purpose so many of us seek, yet fail to achieve.

First of all, Buddhism's focus on attentiveness and mindfulness is a wonderful antidote to denial. Our first line of defense in dealing with difficult issues, denial can have devastating effects.

Denial of an addiction, denial of a relationship problem, denial of personal shortcomings, denial even of death—it is a demon with many forms. As in overcoming fear, we must first of all accept its existence—we must not deny denial itself. When we can do that, we have taken the first step in overcoming whatever problem we have been trying to avoid.

Being mindful and aware, being really awake, does more than break down the doors of denial. It also keeps us focused on the present. And if we are focused on this moment, we won't be dwelling on the past. We won't be in the land of guilt, regret, and revenge. Nor will we be thinking pointlessly about the future—a land of uncertainty. The present moment, with all its potential for beauty and opportunity, is a much better place to dwell, and the only place we can ever really be.

THE GREAT AWAKENING

Another great example of how Buddhism can be helpful in everyday life is the way it helps us create a sense of perspective. The belief, for instance, that there is no self helps put into perspective our significance in the greater scheme of things. It helps us realize that this world, and whatever is beyond, can get on very well with or without us—that we are in fact, such little things when the stars come out. And knowing this certainly puts things in perspective, reminding us that we really don't need to take ourselves or life in general too seriously. There is in fact a good reason for that big Buddhist smile.

One of the basic human challenges is learning to let go. Here again Buddhism comes to the rescue. Almost daily, in some way or other, we are called on to let go. To let go of our children as they mature, of spells of anger, of resentment and hurt. We are called on to let go of our own self-identity as we evolve and move through the stages of life. We have to let go of memories, both good and bad, and accept that change and impermanence are part of our lives.

Buddhism also reminds us that the opposite of letting go—craving, grasping, clinging—leads inevitably to disappointment and unhappiness. Even when what we desire is a good thing—such as love, for instance—we must accept that it won't last forever, unchanged, contrary to the words of many popular songs.

But perhaps the most important thing that Buddhism can teach us is the art of living according to the Middle Path, of living life to the full without attachment, seizing each moment, keeping in step with its eternal rhythm.

This, after all, is how the Buddha himself lived. After he attained Enlightenment he remained fully engaged with his community, his neighbors, his followers, with the world around him.

But he was attached to none of it, not even to life itself. This is the secret of living a Buddhist life.

Cultivating awareness, of mindfulness, through Vipassana meditation is without doubt one of the most effective ways of mastering that secret. It's effective because by applying ourselves conscientiously and diligently to its practice, meditation will help us let go.

It's all in the mind

We can all learn from the story of the
fantastic but troubled mathematician John
Nash, even though we may never attain his
brilliance

Only now are scientists begin-
ning to fully appreciate the power of the mind. In medicine,
for example, they witness its incredible healing power.
They accept this power as a very special, intangible force,
yet they still do not understand fully what it is, or how it
works.

Perhaps first we should ask ourselves what we mean
when we refer to the mind. "It's all in the mind," we say.
But where is our mind? Our brains help us use our minds
on a physical level but we know that our brain and our
mind are not one and the same. "By the mind of man we

understand that in him which thinks, remembers, reasons, wills," is one definition. "The intellectual or rational faculty in man; the understanding; the intellect; the power that conceives, judges, or reasons; also, the entire spiritual nature; the soul," is another.

However we define the mind, we all know that it is our mind that defines us. It determines who we are and what we are. A core Buddhist belief says, "Mind is the master. With the mind everything is possible." Another saying, "Mind is the master, body is the slave," reminds of this basic wisdom.

How then can we use the infinite power of our minds to lead a richer, more meaningful life? We can learn much to help us from the discourses of the Buddha. "I know not of any other single thing so intractable as the untamed mind. The untamed mind is indeed a thing intractable." But this is followed by, "I know not of any other single thing so tractable as the tamed mind. The tamed mind is indeed a thing tractable."

Speaking to an audience of monks, the Buddha continued, "I know not of any single thing that brings such woe as the mind that is untamed, uncontrolled, unguarded, and unrestrained. Such a mind indeed brings great woe." But then he said, "I know not of any single thing that brings such bliss as the mind that is tamed, controlled, guarded, and restrained. Such a mind indeed brings great bliss."

The film *A Beautiful Mind,* in which Russell Crowe gave such an impressive performance, is based on the true story of John Nash, a brilliant American mathematician, who was the recipient of the 1994 Nobel Prize for Economics. His ground-breaking proposition, the Nash Equilibrium, changed aspects of economic theory that had been taught for centuries. Given his accomplishments, it's hard to believe that he spent his life struggling with schizophrenia.

He had his own way of dealing with the world, explaining natural phenomena with his unusual grasp of mathematics. Refusing to attend school, he lived instead in a world he created for himself in his mind. He became increasingly delusional, and the film shows how, with the help of his wife and psychiatric counselling, he finally gained control of his brilliant mind.

We can all learn from the story of John Nash even though we may never attain his brilliance. And the lesson is clear enough. The mind may be the master of the body, but we must learn also to follow the wisdom of the Buddha, "I know not of any other single thing so tractable as the tamed mind," and become master of our mind. We are, after all, what we think we are.

We often talk about wishing to have "peace of mind" as if it is something others can give us, when in fact it can come only from within ourselves. As we begin that process of introspection, we can learn much from these wise "watchwords."

"Watch your thoughts; they become words
Watch your words; they become actions
Watch your actions; they become habits
Watch your habits; they become your character
Watch your character; it becomes your destiny"

Frank Outlaw

Life's simple beauties

Just as rice and curry complement each
other, so mind and body must function
together

The way of life for many people,
particularly for those living in Asia, has changed dramatically
over recent years. Today, more than ever we seem to
be competing with time. "I simply don't have time," is a
common expression. Busy schedules, simply getting to our
place of work at the appointed hour, allow us little space for
ourselves—that private and personal space when we can
take stock of where we are going with our lives, and how we
plan to get there.

Many people will remember that when they were young
they would often accompany their parents or grandparents

to a temple. And they brought rice and curry to offer to the monks. This was a great moment in their young lives; they did it with a pure heart and with respect for the monks, who pass on the Buddha's teachings for us and for others in this life.

Food for monks traditionally includes rice and curry. You would not think to eat either just by itself. They go together, they complement one another. Our mind and the vehicle we occupy in this life—our body—must function together also for us to be a complete person, healthy both in body and mind.

Keeping our mind and body together is not always easy. Sometimes when we are engaged in an everyday task, for example, our mind "wanders," it becomes unfocussed and unguarded—allowing unwanted and unhealthy thoughts of temptation and desire an opportunity to slip in and take over.

The lesson here is clear enough; we should always be mindful. Without mindfulness, even the simplest task in life can become fraught with difficulties. But with mindfulness, when we are truly focused, we can see that even a simple task has a purpose, and because of what it can show us, it also has a beauty of its own.

Continuing with the theme of what we eat, the Buddha warned us not to pay attention to the trimmings, the tempting desserts that we really don't need.

In some cultures mothers will tell their children, "If you don't eat your meat and vegetables, you will not get any dessert." Mothers of course know that meat and vegetables—"rice and curry"—are the most nutritious part of the meal and all that is necessary for the child. They also recognize that temptation, the promise of a favorite dessert, is a powerful incentive for the child to first eat what's good for him or her.

As adults, when we are mindful, we will find that rice and curry is enough for each meal. We will no longer yearn for the dessert. We will find that maintaining a constant harmony of our body and mind, a balance between what our body needs and what our mind desires, will give us the ability to live this life with a sense of contentment.

That contentment, and the sense of fulfillment it brings, comes from within ourselves. We no longer need the short-lived pleasures of life's desserts, pleasures that always have their price. Without their temptation, we will continue to develop as a well-rounded human being. We become more and more capable of finding contentment within our own minds and through our own wisdom. We no longer need to look for external happiness, and as we develop, our social and physical freedom will be preserved and strengthened.

Think of a mother and a demanding child. While walking down the street, they pass by a toy shop which has a very expensive toy. The mother has little money to spare, but the child, as children do, drags her into the shop. That toy is the most important thing in the life of the child at that moment, and finally, perhaps for the sake of peace and quiet, the mother gives in and buys the toy she can ill afford.

The next day that toy is in pieces, discarded by the child as something of no more interest. The pleasure it brought was transitory but the hardship it would cause, the strain on the family budget, would be long-lasting.

As adults, we generally put aside childish things, but we can still be distracted by temptations when our mind and body are not in harmony. Maintaining mindfulness, being aware of the moment, will help us resist the temptation of life's desserts. When we follow the teachings of the Buddha we will know that rice and curry are enough of themselves, and that one should always accompany the other.

Idle curiosity

It sounds harmless but it can in fact be quite
damaging

"Don't think too much. If you
do you will go crazy." We have probably all heard this
advice on more than one occasion, and so far as it applies
to others, it seems eminently sensible.

People are usually trying to tell us, "Look, I know you're
just trying to get to the bottom of it, but it's not really so
important is it? Why do you need to know who the woman
in the photo is? If she's not his wife as you believe, why
does it matter? It could be another relative, one of his
staff. There are any number of possibilities. It might even
be his wife with a facelift and a new hairdo. Let's just have
another coffee." We know that's good advice and we do
our best to follow it, but even as we sip our coffee, our idle

curiosity nudges at us yet again . . . who is that woman anyway?

Idle curiosity. That's a good description of something that sounds harmless but which can in fact be quite damaging. First we need to be aware that it's quite different from the Mother of Invention and Discovery—the inquiring mind—which involves searching for the truth, discovering for example how a particular natural phenomenon occurs through a process of reasoning, logic, inspiration, and a touch of the Edisonian perspiration. Yes, we do need to work at it sometimes when we're looking for answers, but as writer Cindi Myers stylishly points out, "Without the one percent of inspiration, all the perspiration in the world is only a bucket of sweat."

Can we now see at least one reason why idle curiosity can be damaging? There's clearly little perspiration involved and certainly no inspiration—it's idle. And usually it's counter-productive, sending our minds off in a dozen tangents—could it be this, or perhaps that? It can lead to gossip, scandal-mongering, and baseless speculation. Better by far for us to get on with the task at hand than to give in to what could be called curiosity doodling. If we clutter our mental desktops with trash loads of trivia, there'll be no room for those vital flashes of inspiration so essential to the continuum of discovery and revelation.

There is of course another, more fundamental dimension to all of this mental meandering and that is the imperma- nence of all things and the need for us to see things as they really are. This leads to what is described in early Buddhism as *Upekkha* "equanimity," or "inner peace." When we see things as they truly are, there is no longer a separation between us and reality. We see without illusion. Seeing this way gives us peace with ourselves, peace with one another, peace with the whole universe.

When we look for the Buddha within us we are acknowledging the profound reality that we are hoping to awaken in ourselves. To succeed, we need to step beyond our ordinary consciousness, not in the intellectual sense, but by allowing our intuition to guide us in the direction of the truth, compassion, and wisdom of Dharma.

Easier said than done? Yes, it is, and we certainly will never succeed by indulging in idle curiosity. How then do we take that step beyond our "natural" thought processes to a deeper understanding? How can we get closer to the truth without becoming mired in doubt and disappointment?

We can start by accepting the inescapable truth of impermanence, of selflessness, and of what is commonly referred to as suffering, but which perhaps more accurately can be described as "not functioning properly"—"being off center." The acceptance of these three basic truths will usher in a life of genuine humility, as we see through the ego and its machinations.

Let's first look at the notion of impermanence. We can view this idea instinctively as something to regret, "Why must beautiful things wither and die? Why cannot those we love and cherish always be with us? Why can't we always be happy? Why can't we live forever? Think though, when we are moved by the suffering of others—the all-too-frequent examples of man's inhumanity to his fellow man, the victims of disease, those afflicted with terrible physical and mental disabilities. Isn't it good then that their suffering will not be permanent?

Acceptance of the concept of impermanence also allows us to fully embrace the Buddha's most fundamental teachings, and that is for us to always live in the moment, and this means taking the rough with the smooth. To revel in the joy of living while accepting the sadness and disappointments that are part of the whole. To be truly mindful of each moment, knowing that even as we do so, it is already passing.

The idea of selflessness has always been difficult for most people to understand and more difficult still to accept. "After all," we say, "I am me. I am not someone else. And even if I am not me, I must still be someone. I know I exist in mind and body so if there is no "I" what is there? Discussions along these lines can be bewildering but we can begin to grasp the notion of selflessness in a relative sense. Poet Hermann Hagedorn captured its essence when he wrote of a starlit sky:

"We are such little men when the stars come out,
So small under the open maw of the night . . .
When the stars come out we are such little men
That we must arm ourselves in glare and thunder,
Or cave in on our own dry littleness."

And what of suffering, of being "off center"? In the practice of Tai Chi, the importance of having "center," both mental and physical, is constantly stressed. Without it you can easily be caught off balance and suffer the consequences.

We began by discussing the not so harmless habit of indulging in idle curiosity. We have looked at impermanence, at selflessness, at suffering and the need to step up to a different level of consciousness—to see the big picture, unimpeded by the trivial nature and pettiness of the I, Me, Mine perspective, and we have seen the wisdom of embracing the moment as it is, even as it makes way for the next.

The admonition not to think too much, to not being concerned with things that are of no consequence, is sensible advice. It does not mean we should stop thinking or searching for the truth in our lives—and while we're at it, of living every moment to the fullest.

A universal message

People the world over can embrace
Buddhism's ideals and benefit from its
wisdom

I recently had occasion, with a
small group of friends, to take a trip to a Buddhist temple
in the countryside. Mingling with the early morning
crowds outside this well-known temple I was struck
by the timeless quality of the image of the long line of
monks winding their way to the hundreds of waiting
almsgivers.

As they came closer I noticed several foreign faces
among their ranks, some clearly young, others apparently
elderly. And seeing them, clearly at ease with their fellows,
composed, and self effacing, I had a sense of quiet elation.
Here the spirit of Dharma seemed to hang in the very air.

I felt privileged to be part of that special Dharma moment as I was reminded of the universality of the Buddha's message.

Although many people may have travelled to other countries, most will probably spend their lives in their own country. Their opinions and attitudes will be shaped by their own cultural and social mores, and because of Buddhism's traditional influence on the national psyche, they may see the Buddha's teachings from a narrow and even nationalistic perspective.

After the chanting, and a spirited interview session with the still feisty elderly abbot, an encounter with a young British couple further reminded me that the very real benefits to be derived from following Buddhist teachings are available to everyone, and that people the world over can embrace Buddhism's ideals and benefit from its wisdom.

Julie was with her husband on holiday "to simply experience a land where Dharma is part of the fabric of society," she said. I took that as a compliment and although I wondered if it were really so, I was impressed by her obvious sincerity and her manner. It was one of quiet conviction. It was clear that Julie wanted to share her experience, and soon, with an occasional prompting from her husband, she explained how she first became interested in *Vipassana* meditation and how, later, it would have a profound effect on her life.

"So how did it all begin?" I asked. Julie smiled and looked at her husband as if seeking his permission to proceed. He smiled back, simply nodding his head as if to say go ahead.

Eager to tell her story Julie explained, "Well I first went to some meditation classes in our home town but the timing was inconvenient, it clashed with my weekly cooking class and I stopped going for a while. Then some new classes started up just a short drive from our house and in a way it really all began from there."

"And did you find them helpful?" I asked. "Yes, very. The classes had a good, supportive atmosphere, very friendly and relaxed. The meditation helped a lot. It made my mind more peaceful for maybe two or three days after the class. But it was a while before I realized that if I meditated every day, I could feel peaceful every day! It began to bring a bit more wisdom into my life."

"Do you think your life has changed much since you began learning about Buddhist meditation?"

"It was a gradual change. At first it was small things, such as becoming a bit more patient and a bit more tolerant. But I think I realized quite quickly that it was what I'd been looking for."

"How do you mean?"

"I wasn't consciously looking for a religion, but I definitely had a feeling of needing some inner strength."

"Inner strength?"

"Yes. At that time my parents were both getting old, and I knew that my father had heart disease and was going to die quite soon. So it was partly worry about how I would be able to cope with his death and support my mother and family that first brought me to the classes."

"What about your family, do you think they were helped as well?"

"Certainly, it helped them a lot over the next couple of years. It helped me to work on improving my relationships with my family. It was probably about two and a half years later that my father actually died, and by that time I felt I had developed a great deal of strength, and could offer a lot of support to my family, especially to my mother. I understood that my own and my family's sufferings were the result of being in *samsara* (cycle of suffering) and that there was a way out."

"When I visited my father for the last time, just before he died in the hospital, I was able to focus more on how I could best help him and my mother come to terms with his impending death. We managed to talk very openly and intimately about our love for each other and to say our farewells."

"And then, after his death, I took part in a special transference of consciousness *puja* (special prayers) for my father with a group of local Buddhists, and also engaged in *Tara* (the female Bodhisattva of compassion) prayers for a few weeks after his death. I found that this helped enormously with the grieving process."

Still gently holding her husband's hand, Julie was leaning against the car that had brought them to the temple. I looked from one to the other. There was no sign of makeup on this young Englishwoman's face yet it had all the radiance of a fresh-faced teenager. Her husband Dennis, always smilingly supportive, and so far, almost silent, seemed completely content.

I returned to my temporary role as interviewer. "How exactly did the *puja* help you?"

"It helped me not to focus on self-pity, but to focus more on my mother's feelings and those of my brother and sister. After the transference of consciousness, I felt completely confident that my father had taken a fortunate rebirth. The night after the *puja* prayers I had extremely vivid dreams of what I took to be pure lands, places of such extraordinary beauty that I'd never actually seen in my waking life. There was a Buddha in it, and all sorts of things! That reinforced my conviction that my father had definitely benefited from the *puja*. I felt very happy."

As Julie seemed about to tell me even more about her progress Dennis finally spoke. Extending his hand he said, "Thank you for listening. We didn't even ask, but we assume you are also a Buddhist."

"Yes, I am, and it's been a great inspiration for me listening to your wife's experiences."

Silent for a moment as her husband ushered her into the car, Julie gave one of her radiant smiles as she looked around at the throng of people leaving the temple grounds. "Great isn't it," she said. "Dharma really works!"

Yes, I thought, as their car crunched over the dusty gravel surface of the car park, it certainly does.

Righteous roots

Practicing morality returns us to the purity of
our original nature

However carefully we follow
the teachings of the Buddha and try to make them part
of our daily lives through the practice of, and in the spirit
of, Dharma, we inevitably face times of doubt and self
questioning. By reminding ourselves of the basic moral
precepts, and seeking and finding answers, we can get
back on track.

Let's think about the basic Buddhist moral precepts that
guide our learning process and shape our development in
Buddhist practice. The Pali term *sila*, which translates roughly
as "morality," also has its own connotations. It denotes a
state of normalcy, a condition that is basically unqualified and
unadulterated. When we practice *sila* we return to our basic

state of untainted purity, our basic human nature where negative influences such as anger, greed, ill will toward others, and jealousy have no place. And as we practice, by being mindful of our emotions as they arise in our daily lives, we are preserving the purity of our human nature.

We must also remind ourselves that on a personal level, the observance of precepts serves as the preliminary groundwork for the cultivation of higher virtues or mental development. *Sila* can be said to be one of the most important steps on the spiritual path. Without morality, right concentration cannot be attained, and without right concentration, wisdom cannot be fully perfected. Thus, morality not only enhances our ethical values, it is crucial to those of us who seek the highest goal of spiritual fulfillment.

Morality is always concerned with the issues of right and wrong, good and evil. For a moral life to be meaningful, these issues must not remain mere theoretical principles, but be translated into practice. Good must be performed, evil must be given up. It is not enough to know what is good or evil, we also need to take proper action with respect to them. We need concrete guidelines to follow, and these are provided by the Buddhist moral precepts. Even the oft-quoted Buddhist ideals of abstention from evil, doing what is good, can be made real simply by doing, by putting those principles into daily practice.

Buddhist moral precepts provide a wholesome foundation for personal and social growth. They are practical principles for a good life and the cultivation of virtues. If we understand the objectives of *sila* and realize its benefits, we will see moral precepts as an integral part of life rather than as a burden to be shouldered. As individuals, we need to train in morality to lead a good and noble life. On the social level, we need to help maintain peace and harmony in society and facilitate the progress of the common good.

As we progress along the path of self-development we inevitably face moral dilemmas. How do we determine what is good and what is not? The opposite of good, for example, may not necessarily be evil; nonetheless, it is usually easy to distinguish right from wrong.

To determine whether an action is good or evil, right or wrong, Buddhist ethics takes into account three factors involved in a karmic action. The first is the intention that motivates the action, the second is the effect the doer experiences as a result of that action, and the third is the effect that others experience as a result of that action. If the intention is good (motivated by love, compassion, and wisdom), and if the result to the doer is wholesome for instance, it helps him or her to become more compassionate and unselfish; and if those to whom the action is directed also experience a positive result, then that action can be considered as good, and beneficial (*kusala*).

If, on the other hand, the action is rooted in negative mental qualities such as hatred and selfishness, if the outcome experienced by the doer is negative and unpleasant, and if the recipients of the action also experience undesirable effects from the action or become more hateful and selfish, then that action is negative and with no benefit (*akusala*).

A particular act may appear to be a mixture of good and bad elements, in spite of the intention and the way it is performed. Thus, an act committed with the best of intentions may not bring the desired result for either the doer or the recipient. Sometimes, an act based on negative intentions may produce seemingly positive results (as stealing can produce wealth). We may confuse one set of actions with an unrelated set of results and make wrong conclusions, or simply misjudge them on account of preconceived social values and traditions. This can lead to misconceptions about the law of karma, and loss of moral consciousness.

Buddhist moral precepts are based on the Dharma, and they reflect such eternal values as compassion, respect, self-restraint, honesty, and wisdom. These are values that are cherished by all civilizations, and their significance is universally recognized.

Moral precepts that are based on such values will always be relevant to human society, no matter to what extent it has developed. So what are these Buddhist guiding precepts?

The first precept admonishes against the destruction of life. This is based on the principle of goodwill and respect for the right to life of all living beings.

The second precept, not to take things which are not given, signifies respect for others' rights to possessions.

The third precept, not to indulge in sexual misconduct, includes rape, adultery, and sexual promiscuity.

The fourth precept, not to tell lies or resort to falsehood, is an important factor in social life and dealings. It concerns respect for truth. The Buddha has said: "There are few evil deeds that a liar is incapable of committing."

The last of the five Buddhist moral precepts enjoins against the use of intoxicants. On the personal level, abstention from intoxicants helps to maintain sobriety and a sense of responsibility.

Socially, it helps to prevent accidents, such as car accidents, that can easily take place under the influence of intoxicating drink or drugs.

The big picture

We must first know ourselves in order to
see the world more clearly

Seeing the big picture, being
able to view our world as if from a fourth dimension in our
minds, is an amazingly effective way of developing what I
would describe as practical Dharma.

I was reminded of this as I returned to Bangkok by air
from a recent upcountry trip. As the plane banked and
prepared for its slow descent, like most window-seat
passengers, I peered through the porthole-like aperture
for a glimpse of the world below. At first all I could see
was part of the wing and a lot of sky. Then, as the aircraft
turned again, quite suddenly there it was—the green and
yellow checkered bedspread of the countryside.

As we descended, the geometric shapes dissolved to show ribbons of roads, the serpentine steel blue of the river, and soon, like a carefully synchronized army of insects, the slow-moving train of vehicles.

From this lofty viewpoint I could see the whole panorama as it unfolded, and for that moment, as the aircraft held its course, the scene below conveyed all the purity and innocence of a child's picture book. I turned away, knowing that image would soon be shattered by the rush of warm air and the jet engine noise of the airport as the doors opened and another plane load of passengers was deposited back on mother earth.

But that "fourth dimension" view, the big picture, stayed with me as I looked out from our taxi at a now rain-soaked Bangkok. Later, as I caught up with the news, it helped me in my understanding as I read of more accounts of man's inhumanity to man.

Pondering all this, and looking at the often graphic television images of the injured and bereaved, I was comforted by the realization that horrific as these events were, they created a mere ripple on a much greater sea of tranquillity and calm. And that sea, that continuum of time and space, of truth, of beauty and love, is in every one of us. Without beginning, without end. It simply is. But to know the big picture, the broad canvas painted with bold strokes and strong, contrasting colors, we must be able to understand the small picture, the details. We cannot hope to achieve that elevated "fourth dimension" unless first we know ourselves.

That's why so much of the Buddha's teachings urge us to take a close look at ourselves. We may think we know a great deal about the world, about everything, and how "it all works" but how much do we know about ourselves, how we work?

To help answer that question, Buddhism has given us two basic methods, both based on meditation—*Vipassana* and *Shamata*. These are commonly described, respectively, as "insight" and "calm abiding" meditation. Although they are often taught, initially, in sequence, with the idea being that first we must learn to calm our minds before we can benefit from the clarity of inner vision we will achieve, the two meditation methods are intended to work together, like one hand washing the other.

If we wish to see what is in a glass of swirling, muddy water, we set the glass down and let the dirt settle. Then we can see at a superficial level what is, and what is not in the water. Taking that analogy further, the contents of the glass need to be analyzed scientifically before all the various constituents can be identified. And that process can go on down to the sub-atomic level and, theoretically, beyond.

The pursuit of knowledge and the ultimate understanding of how things are, can be a joyful process, and ultimately, a joyous experience. When James Watson and Francis Crick discovered the structure of DNA, the basic molecule of life, in 1953, they were of course revealing a truth that had always existed. What they unravelled was a fantastically elegant process of genetic replication that was both immensely exciting and deeply moving as they pondered its implications.

Responding to questions at the time of their momentous discovery, one of the researchers explained, "Carbon-based life forms are replicated by stacks of genes. Gene strands resemble the snakes in the symbol of medicine. A double helix. When one strand separates from the other, both replicate the missing halves."

They were asked, "How do the gene strands replicate themselves?" "Each strand has a molecular sound. This sound attracts the needed element and repels others."

Scientific confirmation indeed for the notion that each life-form has its own vibration. A unique symphony of life.

A baby's laugh creates smiles for the listening parents. Sound has consequence.

As we look inside ourselves to discover our own truth with the help of *Vipassana* we are not seeking to negate all conscious thought, as sometimes is mistakenly believed— that would be pointless. From nothing comes nothing. Instead we seek to listen to the sounds of the universe that are within each one of us. To tune in to the vibrations of the eternal cycle of life and death, to understand the impermanence of all things, save Truth itself.

It was of course through meditation, that the Buddha himself found enlightenment. In the course of his self-imposed introspection he was confronted by the dilemma that suffering in itself brings no more enlightenment than does pleasure.

He was tormented by desires as he contemplated what to do with his life—whether he should return to the vain pleasures of his earlier years, which he now understood to be ultimately pointless, or continue to suffer and deny himself pleasures, even though he now realized that this also brought no meaning into his life.

Suddenly enlightenment came to the prince, and at that moment, he became the Buddha. Realizing both the self-destructiveness of those who deny their desires and the misery of those who follow their desires, the Buddha also saw that there is a Middle Path, which is to simply lose one's desires. That is, an enlightened person should simply exist without desire.

He sees the Big Picture.

A freed mind

Insight meditation teaches us to embrace and
live each moment to the fullest

"I need a break; if I go on like
this I'll have a nervous breakdown." It's something we all
have heard or perhaps said at one time or another. And
often our friends or family members will encourage us.
"Yes, a break will do you good, you'll be all the better for
it, you'll come back rearing to go."

At first glance it seems like good advice. It's certainly
true that new sights and sounds can be quite refreshing, a
change of pace can be very beneficial. But before we make
arrangements for a long weekend at our favorite getaway,
we need to understand what it is we are escaping from.

When we refer to escaping we generally mean gaining our freedom from physical or mental restrictions. Our feeling for the need to escape, even temporarily, is partly the result of life's pressures, but mainly it arises because we are not free in the present moment.

We may well benefit superficially from what we tell ourselves is a well-earned break. Often, though, it is nothing more than a distraction from the daily routine, from the prison we have made in our minds. Even on a comparatively long holiday are our minds truly free? We may be enjoying the moment, the fresh sea breezes; the trek through the leafy forest, but a part of the mind constantly takes us back to our routine environment.

"Will I have time to complete that report when I get back?" "I should have done my tax return before I left."

"And grandmother, she was doing quite poorly, I hope she's OK. I hope they remember to give her her medicine."

What then do we really mean by "being free in the present moment?" It is about being awake to each experience in the moment, and thus consciously embracing life as fully as possible in our everyday experience.

But what is our ordinary, everyday experience? It's not just our awareness of external circumstances or even such ordinary activities as walking, eating, sleeping, breathing, and speaking; it includes also our thinking and feeling: our ideas, moods, desires, passions, hopes, and fears. In its most accessible form, ordinary, everyday experience, is just how we feel at any particular moment.

It is in this moment that we find reality and freedom, for acceptance of life is acceptance of the present, now and at all times. To allow this moment of experience and all that it contains, the freedom to be as it is, to say what it has to say, to come and go in its own time, this is to allow the moment, which is where we always are, to set us free. And one of the ways we can achieve this is to practice Insight Meditation.

"Oh yes, that's something I've been meaning to pursue for a long time, but I'm always too busy. I have my job, then there's my family, and at weekends, there's the tennis club and. . . ." If you're one of the many well-meaning people who responds in such a way when the subject of Insight Meditation is raised, then you are also admitting you have yet to attain the clarity of vision and contentment that comes from "being free in the present moment."

When we practice Insight Meditation we pay clear attention to whatever exists naturally in this present moment. The specific focus for our awareness can vary, from bodily sensations to sights and sounds to thoughts and feelings. Often we begin by paying attention to the sensations of breathing. We turn our attention to the breath and simply experience, in as continuous a way as possible, the physical sensations of breathing in and breathing out. This simple activity, of paying attention to our experience in the present moment, is what the Buddha called "mindfulness." Mindfulness is the heart of Insight Meditation.

But meditation is not restricted to the special surroundings of a meditation center, or even the quiet atmosphere of a special room in our house, it can also be carried on throughout our daily activities. We can be mindful of the movement of the body, the sensations in walking, the sounds around us, or the thoughts and feelings that come into the mind.

And as our meditation practice develops, we find that the mind becomes calmer and clearer. We start to see the influence of our habitual patterns of moods, expectations, hopes, and fears. In seeing through the mind's conditioning, we can live more fully in the present moment with all the benefits of clarity, compassion, and understanding it brings.

This is the first taste of freedom. We are fully in touch with our experience of life, but we are not limited by it. We find we can manage the ups and downs of daily life more easily. We become more tolerant, even in situations where normally we might respond angrily. We begin to see the truth within us.

Does this mean then that by achieving the freedom offered by Insight Meditation we will no longer find the need to take a break from our usual routine? Whether we do or not is entirely up to us, but if we do, it will be simply because we think it's a good idea, not because we are escaping from our own confusion.

Wherever we are, and whatever we're doing, whether relaxing on that breezy seashore, trekking through the forest, or handling a tricky problem at work, we experience it with a free spirit and open heart.

One of the most well-known quotations of the Buddha says, "Do not dwell in the past, and do not dream of the future, concentrate the mind on the present moment." If we do that, the moment will always be ours.

Blind faith

True wisdom means to directly see and
understand for ourselves

Have you ever wondered why it is that what we profess to believe in, what dogmas we follow, especially with regard to religion, seem to be more to do with geography—which part of the world we live in—rather than the result of us having thought things out for ourselves?

Would the millions who follow one faith in a country where that belief is dominant still follow that particular faith had they been born in a country where another religion holds sway? Did they come to their beliefs after careful questioning, after thinking for themselves, or did they simply follow tradition, accepting the teaching of others as the ultimate wisdom?

Dharma teachings

Not questioning what is often presented to us as facts is not restricted to matters of religious faith. Most of us can think of examples of "facts" that we heard as children that we accepted and perhaps, in our ignorance, even now still believe. Ideas about health and medical matters for instance.

Have you ever been advised, perhaps by well-meaning friends to tilt your head back when you have had a nosebleed? Well, since that would have been bad advice, doctors have long advised against what may seem to be a common sense procedure. Tilting your head back can cause the blood to drain into the throat, which may cause choking or vomiting.

Or you may have been told that sudden changes of temperature experienced—for example—by shoppers trudging from one air-conditioned store to the next, or getting a thorough soaking will give you a bad cold or even the dreaded flu.

Not so—colds and flu are caused by a virus; all the available research demonstrates that sudden changes of temperature, or even going outside without thoroughly drying your hair after a shower, have nothing at all to do with it.

Sometimes we believe in things simply because they seem quite plausible, the idea that we'll likely catch a cold after a soaking for instance, or that eating too much sugar will give us diabetes. Together with the half truths and plain falsehoods, there's a mass of misinformation that persists, and seems self perpetuating.

And many people the world over still cling to superstition. Wiser observers may recognize these ideas for what they are and perhaps have fun in ridiculing them; others, who regard themselves as otherwise being rational, seem to be happy to defy logic and still believe there's some truth in such ideas.

"If a black cat walks towards you, it brings good fortune, but if it walks away, it takes the good luck with it." This is a belief common to many cultures in the same category as, "You must get out of bed on the same side that you get in or you will have bad luck," or "If you blow out all the candles on your birthday cake with the first puff you will get your wish."

Superstition, old wives tales, folklore and these days, urban legends, can only exist in our minds when we don't think for ourselves—when we accept what others tell us without questioning. The Buddha encouraged us to question and analyze his teachings because he understood from his own experience that truth, and the wisdom that comes from it, can only be attained by looking for it.

In recent times, there was much debate among national leaders about the rightness or wrongness of going to war against a nation whose leader was perceived as being a threat to international security. On both sides of the argument there was propaganda, misinformation, and the more insidious, disinformation. Although what we think in such matters may have little effect on the outcome, this is an example of an issue where we should weigh carefully what we believe to be the facts and come to our own conclusion.

It is not wisdom if we simply believe what we are told. True wisdom is to directly see and understand for ourselves. It is also to be open to new ideas but to accept or reject them only after careful consideration and then be ever willing to re-examine them. And we must especially be prepared to admit the error of our thinking when we are proven to be wrong.

Achieving that degree of wisdom is not easy. It requires courage, patience, flexibility, and intelligence. It also brings with it great rewards. Without wisdom for example, when we exercise compassion and show loving kindness to others we are simply being kind-hearted fools. The wisdom that comes from right thinking—seeing things as they really are, of accepting the impermanence of all things, allows us to live without the craving that causes suffering and the self delusion that comes from false ideas.

So how do we achieve this wisdom in our everyday lives? Surely it takes time, a great deal of study, and perhaps even a teacher? After all, how can we learn if we don't even know what questions to ask? How can we even begin, when we have to work everyday to support ourselves and our families?

The Buddha would say that the wisdom we seek is within ourselves. If we begin by ridding our minds of selfish desires, this is the first step, not only to escape from suffering, but to allow wisdom to reveal itself. And when it does, we will recognize its truth and purity.

Theory into practice

The means to free ourselves is always there if
we look hard enough

Have you ever noticed that when someone tells you a story, especially if it's offered as a humorous contribution, it is often especially revealing about the storyteller? We have all been surprised for example, when a straight-laced colleague tells a joke, seemingly completely out of character, or when the office clown shows a serious side of his character with a thought-provoking account of a personal incident about which we were all completely unaware.

Usually these "revelations" take place at some get-together when people are feeling in a relaxed mood. Not only entertaining, such occasions are often therapeutic, allowing us to get things off our chest the way an actor does in playing a part. They can also be educational as was a recent weekend away from it all I recently shared with a group of colleagues.

It wasn't a retreat in the meditative sense, although the woodland setting and the rustic accommodations offered an ideal atmosphere for introspection. It was simply meant to be a chance to escape the decibel din and polluted air and to enjoy the real or perceived benefits of sleeping under mosquito nets; of washing in the cool (actually freezing) waters of the nearby stream, and hiking up mountain trails, worn to a slippery smoothness by the rugged footwear of a thousand tourists.

And at the end of the day, that time of aching limbs and weary minds, came the storytelling. There was no escape. Those who attempted to sneak off would be called back to the fold with cries of "Come on, come on. Everybody has to join in."

The unofficial leader of our get-together had wisely ruled that our storytelling session should follow certain loose guidelines. It was therefore decreed and agreed that contributions should have more than just entertainment value. They should, in the long-established tradition of such tales, have a moral.

I thought it would be fun and even instructive if I recounted a couple of the stories as I remember them.

The first concerns a young, highly educated professor of physics who decided he would take time off in the tradition of the seventh-year sabbatical. He would take a sea voyage around the world, exchanging the classroom for the ship's deck. The ocean would be his mentor, the starlit sky, his inspiration.

But he couldn't give up his natural inclination to pass on his wisdom, and every evening he gave a short talk on one subject or another to an audience of passengers and crew. After one talk in which he discussed the importance of oceanography, he was approached by an old sailor. "What's all this about what you call oceanography professor. It's all I can do to pronounce it, let alone understand it."

"Well my good man," said the professor, "it's just one of the many subjects you should master if you make your living as a sailor. What about astronomy for instance, meteorology, and these days, navigation technology?"

"Don't know nothing about any of those things either professor. I never learnt to read or write properly. What I know, I know."

"But you have to understand the science and the theory behind what you do."

"Oh I leave all that to others. All those 'onomies and 'ologies, I'll never get my head round those. Anyway, thanks for your time professor, I've got some work to do before I turn in."

Later that very night, the professor was awakened by a thunderous noise, and seconds after, a frantic knocking on his cabin door. There was the old sailor, holding a life jacket.

"Professor, what do you know about swimology?"

"What? What's going on. What do you mean, swimology?"

"Can you swim professor?"

"Well, of course, I have a comprehensive knowledge of the theory, it's all a matter of . . ."

"But can you swim? The ship's run aground. We've hit a rock, and we're sinking."

The old sailor thrust the life jacket at the blinking academic. "Put this on and follow me. I'll help you into a lifeboat—what you might call survivology."

And the moral of that little tale of the sea is that however much we understand the teachings of the Buddha, of Loving Kindness and Compassion for instance, that knowledge will have no effect on our lives, or the lives of others, unless we put theory into practice.

Here's another tale with a twist, contributed by the oldest member of our group.

In an area where the law was in the hands of a ruling clique who would routinely imprison their opponents on false charges, yet another protester was hauled off in the middle of the night and thrown into the dungeons of the old castle that served as the jail.

"You've got to get me out of here," he said to the only visitor he was allowed, a monk from the local temple. "Be patient, I will bring you something that will help you," said the monk. He had to wait another month for the next visit, but this time his visitor left him a parcel with the words, "Make full use of this, and you will gain your freedom."

Obviously it had been scrutinized by the guards, so he had little hope of it containing anything of much use. And when he saw that it was just a prayer mat, his disappointment quickly turned to anger. What good is this, he asked himself, unless it contains something of practical value, something to blast a hole in the wall for instance, or some high-tech device that would cut through the steel door of his cell. But it was just what it appeared to be—a simple prayer mat.

One day he picked it up and noticed it appeared to have some kind of pattern on it. He studied it carefully, holding it up to the only source of light, a narrow slit in the old castle wall. He could make out only a few faint lines, but they did seem to be part of some kind of diagram.

Over the next many days, spurred by the possibility that the mat contained some kind of secret message, and remembering the monk's words that if he used the mat, he would gain his freedom, he would study it from every angle, but try as he may, he could see only the same faint outline.

"Perhaps I should really use it, after all that's what the monk actually said." So that night, in the semidarkness, he unrolled the mat, and closing his eyes, began to pray for understanding. He remained in silent prayer for a long while and finally opened his eyes. As he did so he saw that the lines on the mat that had been until then, barely discernible, were absolutely clear. They had been drawn in luminous paint. He was looking at a detailed diagram of an escape route accessible from a secret opening in his dungeon wall.

I hardly need point out that the moral here is that for each one of us, however much we feel imprisoned by life's misfortunes and the suffering we must endure, the means to free ourselves is always there if we look hard enough.

Elusive search

**Taking the middle path can help us avoid
conflict and move closer to ultimate truth**

Since the very earliest times,
humanity has wrestled with the concept of truth. It has
occupied the finest minds, and formed the basis of a whole
body of philosophical thinking.

The need for each one of us to be steadfast in our
commitment to leading our lives based on the fundamental
truths of existence, is increasingly important today when
the values that come from that commitment are being
challenged at every level.

How then do we define truth, both in its broadest terms
and how it applies to living and working in the day-to-day
world in which we all must be involved?

At the practical level, we might say truth is the reality of nature, the cycle of birth and death of all living things. The truth of night and day, of heat and cold, of desire and suffering, of sadness and discontentment, and the uplifting truth of joy and understanding that comes from the ultimate truth of love and compassion.

In its broadest sense, we might also say truth is that which is. However, and wherever, we look for truth, it remains unchanged. It is the eternal constant. Paradoxically when we search for the truth, we are not always ready to receive it. If we open our minds in love and a desire to see things as they are, truth will find us.

Opening our minds however, means more than sitting passively in our favorite chair, and saying something like, "Let the truth come in." Rather than having any great revelation, we are more likely to nod off to sleep. First, we need to understand the distinction between Relative Truth and Ultimate Truth.

Relative truth describes what we generally regard as facts—the sun rises in the east, sets in the west, there are seven days in a week, the shortest distance between two points is a straight line, and if we go for a long time without eating, we will feel hungry.

Surely, we might say, those facts and many others that we have come to accept as being indisputable, are more than relative? After all, the sun does rise in the east and does set in the west; we all know that, we can see it with our own eyes. The answer of course is that such truths are relative because the way we perceive them relates to our own experience.

The sun only appears to rise and fall as it does because of its relative position to the earth; days, months, weeks, years are only terms we have evolved to provide a way of communicating ideas about the passage of time. Relative truths such as these and the millions of others that exist, form a vast interdependent network, a framework of information and knowledge that serves as an essential source of reference for us to manage our lives.

Although we clearly need this bank of information, of relative truths, to be able to function in today's world, we must also remind ourselves that those truths exist only in relation to one another, that they have no real identity, no actual existence in themselves.

What then of Ultimate Truth, does that exist? Simply by searching for it we acknowledge that it exists, our search itself is part of the Ultimate Truth. Does this mean that to lead a happy and fulfilling life we should devote ourselves to discovering the Truth? If we wish to pursue such a course, we are free to do so, and we need look no further than within ourselves.

Nevertheless, whether we spend every thinking moment exploring the profound questions of our existence and the nature of reality, or think only of such imponderables in moments of quiet contemplation, or in the few minutes before our favorite television program, the truth is always there for us to see. And when we do see the truth, we will realize that by constantly searching for a meaning in life we are actually creating the opposite—a state of confusion leading to suffering and unhappiness.

We are often reminded that the Dharma of the Buddha is one of a middle way and we may think of this as meaning that we should avoid extremes of behavior, of clinging too much to one pleasure or another—that we should "take the middle path." This is certainly a valid interpretation, but by advocating the middle way, the Buddha also meant that we should reject the extremes in the way we think about the meaning of our existence and the way this too can affect our daily lives.

We tend to think, for example, of people being good or bad and may say that people are basically good or we may express the opposite and say that people are basically evil.

Neither of these views represents reality, they are simply ideas, concepts. Clearly, taking the middle path is more logical; it is also closer to reality.

For us to begin fearlessly to take the middle path we must truly accept the reality of truth as the arising and ceasing of existence as it is as this moment. When we grasp that reality, we will see that the confusion that arises in our search for that elusive truth becomes irrelevant, and once free from that confusion, we become a step closer to achieving the ultimate freedom that comes from seeing things as they really are.

So what does all this mean to us in this world today? How will an understanding of reality help us to cope when even now, conflicts continue to threaten the lives of people and the very existence of independent nations?

A clear understanding of the Buddhist concepts of Relative and Ultimate Truths will allow each one of us to realize that those very conflicts arise from reasoning based on Relative Truths and thus have no foundation in reality.

Dharma in the workplace

Shallow society

An obsession with looks distracts from the
true meaning of life

One of the most beautiful faces
I have seen recently belonged to a young lady in my office
who had returned from a ten-day *Vipassana* meditation
retreat. She had been troubled by many personal problems,
both imagined, and to her at least, very real.

Like many young women of her age she tried to make
herself look as attractive as possible. A bit on the plump
side, she was an avid follower of all the latest slimming
fads, trying out facial creams and other beauty preparations.
Sadly, none of them seemed to work for her. In fact, the
application of one particular lotion caused a reaction which
required medical attention.

Naturally, she became depressed, which in turn caused her to become irritable and bad tempered. In short, she became unattractive externally, both physically and from the point of view of her personality. Internally, she was tormented by emotions of dissatisfaction, frustration, and finally, self-loathing. And, perversely, she turned to food for comfort—cakes and pastries, candies and cookies soon became her daily diet.

My first reaction was a desire to help, but especially as a man, I knew I would have to tread carefully. I also knew that basically she would describe herself as a Buddhist while probably admitting she gave only lip service to the teachings of the Buddha.

One day I resolved to put my compassion into practice. "There's a great new vegetarian restaurant opened just around the corner. Come on, let's try it out for lunch." Although she protested, she finally gave in, and soon I had her more or less to myself in the restaurant which was not yet very busy.

I began with what I hoped was a tactful way of getting to the point of my little ruse. "Tell me, how would you define beauty?" "Look, I know you're trying to cheer me up," she said, trying her best to look grateful, and giving me a halfhearted smile. "You're going to tell me that beauty is actually more than skin deep and I should start thinking all kinds of beautiful thoughts, have a good night's sleep and I'll wake up looking like a fresh-faced teenager."

It was my turn to smile, in fact I chuckled loudly. "Well not exactly, although I would certainly say that external beauty can only come from within. We really are what we think. And clearly how we perceive ourselves makes all the difference as to how we appear to others."

"So you're saying to look beautiful, I have to think of myself as being beautiful," "Yes, but there's more to it than that. We've already mentioned that old saying about beauty being only skin deep. Let's look at another adage, the one about beauty being in the eyes of the beholder. Don't you think we can apply this to so many different types of beauty, apart from the obvious physical kind?"

We were half way through our lunch, but I was now beginning to gain her full attention. We talked about the beauty of the arts, of painting, of music, of literature, and of knowledge itself. "Real beauty," I said, "comes from within. It is the beauty of Dharma in body, speech, and mind."

We talked more on this theme, and soon my young colleague was coming up with examples of her own. "You know there's an old noodle seller in the street where I live. I see her almost every day and she always seems to have a smile on her face, even when she has no customers. She must be over 80, but her face has a sort of radiance. I often wonder what she's got to be happy about. She looks like she's just won the lottery." "And I bet she doesn't wear makeup," I chipped in.

It would soon be time to get back to the office but I knew most of my Dharma work was done. In the foyer of the restaurant there was a large mirror and as we left I took my colleague's arm and steered her gently towards its compelling presence. "Do me a favor, take a look at yourself in the mirror and tell me what you see." Smiling slightly, she did as I asked. Even as she studied her reflection she could not prevent the smile developing into a wide grin, and finally a happy laugh.

As we walked back to the office she suddenly tugged my arm, "You know what, you got me thinking and talking so much I forgot to eat my dessert and it was my favorite— carrot cake and creamy sauce."

From the very next day we all noticed a marked change in our young colleague's demeanor. Although she still bore the signs of the allergic reaction on her face, she appeared much less concerned. She seemed to radiate a sort of quiet optimism and was almost determinedly cheerful.

A week later she came to see me. "It's my turn to treat you to lunch, what do you fancy?" We settled for noodles and soon we were trying to catch each other's words over the lunchtime clatter and conversation buzz of the noodle shop. "I have something to tell you. Actually you're the first to know—I haven't even told my parents yet."

Perhaps she's about to get married, or leave to work abroad, I thought. "Well after our discussion last week about beauty, I realized that I had got it all wrong. You know, I read about some of the extreme lengths some people go to achieve what they perceive as beauty, and I felt I wanted to rush out and tell them how misguided they are."

"Is that what you wanted to tell me?" "No, that's just how I feel. You know I have a couple of weeks holiday coming up, well I've decided to use it to go on a meditation retreat. I am putting your advice into practice."

I was of course flattered, but most of all thrilled. My gentle prodding had helped bring her back to the path of self realization, the rest, as they say, would be up to her.

A few weeks later I heard a slight cough, and when I looked up, there she was. Yes, she was slimmer, but the most apparent change was in her face. She appeared at once serene, yet radiant. Quite simply, beautiful. Her inner happiness was clearly evident as she smiled and handed me a single apple.

"For your dessert," she said.

Millionaires seldom smile

Giving to others should always be done
without expecting anything in return

"Who wants to be a millionaire?"
The title of that old song often comes to my mind as I ob-
serve the people that make up what most of us refer to as
high society. It's probably fair to say that you don't have to
be a millionaire or even very rich to be a high-so celebrity.
It's probably also true to say that having money certainly
helps.

You know how it is. You remember the first few lines
of a song and because they touch a chord somewhere in
your psyche, you often sing them to yourself like a mantra,
especially if the tune is also catchy.

"Who wants to be a millionaire, wallow in champagne, have a fancy yacht and a supersonic plane . . ." I was singing thus quietly to myself at a particular glittering gathering when a colleague sidled up and cheekily added his own version of the next line, "I do, I do," he sang, and moved away smiling, before I could say a word.

A while later, I spotted him again. He was still smiling, and when he saw me he beckoned me over. He nodded to a particularly attractive and elegant young woman across the room. "Money can't buy me love . . ." he began. We both enjoyed the joke.

It's also been said that money cannot buy happiness or health, and I was thinking of this old adage and the many others associated with this most basic of human needs when I got home.

How does the idea of making money equate with my Buddhist beliefs? After all, we need money to survive and what can be wrong in creating wealth, a strong, prosperous society, with equal opportunities for everybody? With these ideas running through my mind I decided to look up a few facts about millionaires. The first thing I did was to turn to the actual lyrics of that song that started me off earlier in the evening.

To my surprise, far from singing the praises of the life of a millionaire, the light-hearted lyrics by Cole Porter actually do the opposite. "Who wants a fancy foreign car? I don't. Who wants to tire of caviar? I don't." are typical of the lines of the song.

And as to miserable and reputedly, miserly millionaires, there seems to have been plenty of them around in the past, and these days it also seems that the more millionaires there are, the less merry they become. It's not surprising when we think about it. As people make more and more money, they are able to surround themselves with the material wealth they have long yearned for. A luxurious house, servants, not one, but several cars, all the latest gadgets—it's a familiar scenario.

Often they are proud of their material success and show off their expensive lifestyle. And often too, they become attached to their possessions, so much so that they are in constant fear they may lose them. They become prisoners of their avarice. There are also the miserly millionaires who, in spite of their wealth, never tip, pay their staff the least they can get away with, and spend little, even on themselves.

Such were a family I read of who, although they had received a huge inheritance from their parents, spent very little of it. The six sisters and one brother lived in the same house for 50 years. None of them married and when the last sister died, the estate was valued at hundreds of millions of dollars. Her only dress was one that she had made herself, and she had worn it for 25 years.

It's clear enough that a life spent entirely in the pursuit of wealth in the form of material possessions can leave little time for much else. So, we need to see money for what it really is—a means to an end, not the end itself. The end we seek to achieve will vary with our circumstances, but it should always be to live a happy and contented life, showing generosity and kindness to others—and we don't need to be a millionaire to do that.

Here's a quote I came across which I believe sums up neatly what money can, and cannot, do for us. "Money will buy a bed but not sleep; books but not brains; food but not appetite; finery but not beauty; a house but not a home; medicine but not health; luxuries but not culture; amusements but not happiness."

Not so long ago, a prominent Buddhist temple was in the news for what some described as commercialization of the traditional practice of merit making. Followers, it was said, were being encouraged by the use of modern advertising techniques to donate as much money as possible to the temple to pay for elaborate buildings. A well-known academic commented at the time, "What's the real purpose in going to the temple, to be peaceful in mind, or to see a sort of splendid construction, or colorful architecture? Why pay so much? Remember "merit" does not mean giving your money."

Giving to others should always be done without expecting anything in return. We can give in many ways, including offering our services, providing material gifts, or donating money itself. Giving also requires that it be done with a pure heart, and this means being glad to give before giving, believing in giving while actually giving, and taking delight afterwards in having given. Merit comes not from the giving or the gift, but from the intention of the giver.

And those millionaires? Here's what two old-time ones had to say. "I was happier when doing a mechanic's job," said Henry Ford. From Andrew Carnegie—"Millionaires seldom smile."

Dharma at work

The need to cultivate relationships is based
on mutual respect

Most of us spend a great proportion of our adult life in some form of employment, and whether we run our own business, work for a small or large company, or even work from a "home office," we need to be able to get along with other people. They may be our office colleagues, the company managing director, the cleaning lady, or our customers—they are all people we have to relate to in a work environment, and how we handle our relationships with each one of them can make all the difference between harmony and strife.

The typical office environment is one in which many of us have first-hand experience, and it often seems to take up a disproportionate part of our life. We get in early to avoid the traffic, to impress the boss, to set a good example, or to simply get the work done, and increasingly we leave late, often for the same reasons.

And as we become more and more resentful at how work and all its problems seem to be taking over our lives, we begin to ask ourselves, "Is it all worth it? Why am I doing this?" Often the answer is that we appear to have no choice. We need the money we say, and resign ourselves to what has become a daily drudge.

Clearly there's something wrong. Life shouldn't be like that, and it doesn't have to be. Many, if not most of the work-related problems we face in the office and other work-related environments are about relationships, specifically relationships which are not working properly and which cause disharmony, distress and all round dissatisfaction. In other words, people problems. How we get on with one another.

People who make a living from giving advice on how other people should best be managed in the work environment used to ask questions about whether a particular individual was a good team player, able to work on their own initiative, and respect the views of others. Now they talk about E.Q.—Emotional Quotient. For years most of us have been familiar with I.Q. which refers to our Intelligence Quotient—our ability to comprehend and understand factual knowledge, our verbal and mathematical skills, our memory, and powers of logical reasoning.

The now fashionable E.Q. refers to our ability to deal with emotions and feelings in others, and ourselves, which is the basis of all human relationships. The present thinking is that E.Q. is a better predictor of success in life and work than I.Q. In conventional psychological terms this may well be so, but however accurately it describes our emotional skills, isn't it just another way of describing what I prefer to call "Dharma at Work" and the benefits of its practical application?

In today's global working environment the many work-related problems often stem from the inevitable diverse cultural attitudes that exist between people from different countries and backgrounds. Situations that are tolerated or which are manageable in a social context can lead to a crisis in a business environment. This problem of different cultural attitudes goes much deeper than understanding what might be described as the subtleties of social etiquette in the office context, a subject regularly covered in the business columns of newspapers where the conventional wisdom of mutual understanding and tolerance is the order of the day. We have to do more than simply attempt to develop mutual understanding. We need to cultivate relationships based on mutual respect.

Let's first look at some of the common sources of office conflict and disharmony. Broadly speaking, they can be thought of as colleague problems, and boss problems.

Boss problems are the more difficult to deal with. There's the bossy boss, the aloof and unfriendly boss, and the too friendly boss, the slave-driving boss and the boss who's never there when needed. Then perhaps worst of all, there's the boss who is always the first to arrive, the last to leave and who makes it clear that everybody else is expected to do the same. The implication being that those that don't will be considered as being disloyal.

There's not enough space here to explore specific problems and how to deal with them, but let's look at one real life example that I witnessed in the early days of my own career.

The managing director of the company was of the "first to arrive, last to leave" type. He was also set in his ways, wary of new ideas, believed he knew best, and even in discussion with senior employees, would treat their views with derision and sarcasm. Those who were daring enough to leave at the normal time would be subjected to an icy stare or comments such as, "Before you go to your party, please make sure you complete the report you're working on."

And it was one of those senior employees, "David," who had earlier been very supportive of the managing director and provided valuable assistance in dealing with the company's clients, who finally decided enough, was enough. He began to come into the office late in the day, eventually saying he preferred to work from home. When this didn't work out, he left.

A few weeks after he had left the company I caught up with him at a business event and he seemed eager to share his feelings of being treated badly by someone with whom he had once enjoyed a friendly working relationship. He seemed hurt, and even angry, saying that he hoped others would not share his fate.

Back in the office, the routine of work went on much as usual, but I did notice that the boss was more subdued. He seemed determined to work even harder but appeared to have decided to be less critical of others. It wasn't a happy atmosphere, but there was less tension, and when it was time to go home at the end of the day people would leave without drawing comment.

Then one day, quite unexpectedly, David walked in and knocked on the door of the managing director's office. We heard the "Come in," and the door closed.

Later we heard that David had decided it was not sensible or right for either of them to harbor such mutual ill feelings and that they had agreed they had both been at fault and resolved to re-establish their friendly relationship. He never did come back to work in the office, but the results of his initiative were clear to see in the much better attitude of the managing director.

Whatever level of E.Q. David's initiative represented, for me it was a very clear example of Dharma at work—in both senses of the word.

Dealing with the dragons at work

A friendly, team approach will often work
wonders

There's something about say-
ing "Good morning," especially to colleagues at work, that
seems to present a real problem for some people. This is
particularly true it seems for bosses, by which I mean anybody at any level with authority over others. It's all part of
what I call the po-faced syndrome, and it seems to afflict
managers and supervisors particularly severely.

You know the scenario. A group of workers pauses,
to exchange a few pleasantries or to share a joke, when
their immediate boss gives them a disapproving glare or
perhaps delivers an ultimatum about a certain task having
to be completed on time. "You can sit around gossiping all

day, but that report has to be on my desk by nine o'clock tomorrow morning, even if you have to work all night."

The negative effects of this attitude are obvious, and it's a puzzle why those who behave that way cannot see how counter-productive it really is. The first thing that happens is that those who have been chastised feel resentful. They return to their work muttering among themselves and harboring unpleasant thoughts about their boss, perhaps even agreeing not to finish the job on time just to pay him back.

How different then had the boss greeted them with a smile and said something like, "Good morning everyone. You all seem to be in a cheerful mood. By the way please don't forget we have a nine o'clock deadline for this job tomorrow morning. Let me know if you run up against any problems. Anyway you've made a good start. See you all later."

Apart from being friendly, positive, and encouraging by using a phrase such as "we have a nine o'clock deadline," this approach makes it clear that everyone, including the boss, is part of the same team with a common objective. It also confirms that help will be available if any problems arise. Clearly, this is the right kind of motivation. To be really effective however, it must also be sincere and not just smooth talk turned on when necessary to get the job done. That old adage about being able to fool some people some of the time is simply not true. No one is fooled by insincerity, except perhaps those who indulge in it.

Fortunately, the po-faced syndrome is not always what it seems. How often have we regarded a person to be surly, unfriendly, and even hostile, to discover that they are in fact none of these but simply shy?

There was Arthur for example, the security guard at a company I once worked for. Always serious looking, with the air of a parade ground sergeant-major, he would make everyone feel uncomfortable simply by appearing on his rounds or being at his post when we left the building. We all accepted he had an important job to do, but we wished that just once in a while he would behave less like a robot and more like a human being.

Then one weekend, I bumped into him almost literally in the supermarket. That was the first time I had seen him out of uniform and it was quite a shock. He had two lively young children with him and he appeared to be doing the family shopping. I couldn't avoid saying something. He had obviously seen me.

"Hello Arthur, lovely looking children. Are they yours? From its usual mask of impassive politeness, his face changed instantly into that of a proud father, the friendly neighbor, and a man you would want to be your friend.

With a broad smile he said, "They are indeed—bit of a handful, but I bring them here every Saturday while my wife goes to her coffee morning."

We chatted happily for a while about nothing in particular before getting on with our own Saturday shopping chores. As I left the store I could see Arthur studying the shelves in his typical methodical way while keep a fatherly eye on his children. This time though, there was a difference. He was still displaying that proud and happy smile.

The next Monday morning, encouraged by our Saturday encounter I felt bold enough to venture a, "Good morning Arthur, how are you today?"

There was that smile again and the friendly reply. "Very well sir, and thank you for asking." Arthur's secret was out. He was simply an old softie who gave the impression of being a real terror because he felt that was what his job demanded.

The point here is that many of the dragons we encounter at work are not all what they seem, and those that are unpleasant and bossy can be tamed with understanding and compassion.

Whatever drives their behavior, whether it's a genuine desire to get the work done or part of their own personal career strategy, it is caused by their own lack of confidence. They believe that being anything other than a tough slave driver is the only way. Showing any form of friendliness to those under their authority would, in their eyes, be a sure sign of weakness.

Changing their attitude is not easy, but it's always worth the effort. And what's the big secret to this magical metamorphosis?

Charm, cheerfulness, and a large helping of compassion.

Charm, because even surly, unfriendly and domineering bosses do respond to sincere flattery. "Do you have a few minutes? We would really appreciate your advice on how to approach this job. We know you've had a lot of experience in this area…"

Cheerfulness, because if the dragon approach is met with a cheerful, "Actually with your help we plan to have the whole job finished by this afternoon," the fire will soon fizzle out. And compassion, because those with the po-faced syndrome generally have many problems of their own, not least insecurity and low self esteem.

Remember, a cheery "Good morning," works wonders, both for those to whom it is directed and the person who volunteers it. By the way, there's also nothing stopping you offering an equally cheery, "See you tomorrow," at the end of the working day.

I'm sure Arthur would approve.

Maximum benefits

The Lord Buddha offered sound economic
advice in his teachings

Every day we are bombarded
with information about economics. Every newspaper has
pages devoted to it, every television or radio newscast
includes some sort of business section where the latest
economic developments around the world are discussed
and analyzed.

Immersed in our daily lives, most of us will take little
interest in talk of balance of payments, inflation, cost
of living indices and the like. We may well believe that
economics has little to do with us, and even, that as
Buddhists, we should not be concerned with such things,
viewing the whole world of business as unwholesome—
something to be avoided.

The reality of course, is that we cannot avoid it. Whatever we do, however simply we live, each one of us is an integral part of the system. If we cannot escape the all-embracing consequences of what is now referred to as the science of economics, can we adopt its principles to reflect our Buddhist beliefs? Can there in fact, be such a thing as Buddhist Economics?

If we accept that economics is in fact a science, should it not play a major role in benefiting humanity, helping to create prosperous and harmonious societies, bringing stability, and an acceptable standard of living to all? Obviously the answer is yes, it should, and equally obviously, we can see that it fails to do that. In fact, in many countries around the world, bad economic management results in poverty, with the consequent social unrest and disorder.

Conventional economics fails because its objectives are narrow and take no account of ethical values. To an economist, a bottle of whisky and a book advocating the application of Buddhist principles in business have the same economic value. The potential damaging effects of alcohol to individuals and society in general or the benefits of Buddhist-based business policies, play little or no part in the decision to open a liquor store or a bookshop.

From a Buddhist perspective, economics cannot be viewed as a specialist area of knowledge. Rather it must be see as one of a number of interdependent disciplines working in concert towards the common goal of social, individual and environmental well-being.

Long before economics evolved as a "science," the Buddha set out several principles for sound economic practice, and even in today's world of multi-national corporations and macro-economics, they still hold true, and can be applied equally to big business or to our individual situations.

The first of these principles says that when we work to acquire wealth we must do it in an ethical way, not taking advantage of others or engaging in work or business that is not "Right Livelihood," that is in other words "Unwholesome." Included in this list for example, would be trading in arms and weaponry, trading in people, selling live animals to the slaughterhouse, trading in alcohol and other intoxicants, and making a living out of charging interest on loans.

We could probably add several more to this list but we hardly need reminding that right now in most countries around the world, all of these types of businesses play a major part in the various economies of the countries where they thrive.

Community leaders regularly urge everyone to do their bit in helping to combat the menace of drugs. It's a message that's increasingly directed at those who suffer most from it—the end users. No business can survive without customers.

Young people especially, should be encouraged to follow the Eightfold Noble Path and live their lives according to the Five Precepts. This simple act alone will ensure there are no more customers for the drug peddlers.

The second of the Buddha's economic principles concerned the importance of careful conservation of the money and wealth we acquire. Of the wisdom of putting some aside for a "rainy day"—of spending our money wisely and not on an extravagant and self-indulgent lifestyle.

Living within one's means is the thrust of the third principle. Today, when so many young people get themselves into debt by overspending with their credit cards, this common sense dictum is especially relevant.

The fourth bit of sound advice from the Buddha is to cultivate a network of the "right" kind of friends in our lives. The importance of this virtue was stressed by the Buddha who, especially in the context of economics, taught that simply acquiring, storing, and using wealth is not good enough. We have to build up a network of good people to work with too, before we get around to using our wealth. The Buddha also emphasized that in earning our living, we should try to avoid associating with those who break the Precepts.

The advice the Buddha gave on matters relating to economics was amazingly practical even to the extent of recommending how the family budget should be divided and managed. One part should be reserved for the needs of the family and household, one to extend generosity to our friends, one part to be saved for that rainy day or an emergency, one for charitable causes, and one towards supporting monks.

But, you might say, some people hardly earn enough to survive, how can they possibly begin to even think about saving? Some are driven to stealing or other types of crime simply to feed their children. You feel sorry for them you say, and warming to your theme, you blame the government, citing the low pay of officials such as members of the police force for the rampant corruption we read about almost daily. Think again; do you really believe that stealing, and seeking and accepting bribes can be justified simply because an individual wants more, more than he or she can afford?

Fortunately, there are still those stories that literally show the other side of the coin. Of diligent hard-working parents doing the most menial of jobs and living in the most simple circumstances who struggle each day to feed, clothe, and educate their children, instilling in them the virtues of honesty, truthfulness—of Right Living. They manage what money they have wisely, and sometimes are even able to help others.

Their economic management is based on sound principles, the principles of Buddhist Economics.

The best policy

The practice of honesty and integrity lies at
the heart of the principle of Right Speech

"Corporate America under siege,"
"Big business in big trouble," "Dishonest accounting practices rife," proclaimed the headlines, and we all know they
were referring to the blight of scandals that shook US business, with repercussions that would reverberate around
the world.

And oddly, most observers at the time seemed not
at all surprised. "Business is like that," they would say,
almost as if attempting to justify all the lying, stealing, and
rampant dishonesty. It's easy enough to understand that
attitude. It's all around us. How many times have we heard
the expression, "It's nothing personal, it's just business,"
implying that disregard for the principles of honesty,

integrity, and fairness, is acceptable because, well, it's business.

Under this "It's only business," umbrella of "acceptable" practices, hypocrisy and humbug are the order of the day. While proclaiming an unswerving commitment to noble principles, businesses large and small, continue to exploit employees, paying them minimum wages, and even in extreme cases using children and illegal immigrants as virtual slaves. They pay lip service to conserving the environment while releasing toxic waste into rivers and streams, they falsify invoices and receipts to cheat on their taxes, and in supreme irony, they can be seen making grand public gestures of charity.

Many of us, while despairing at what seems to be an ever growing conspiracy to seek to prosper at the expense of others, ask ourselves what can we do about it. After all, we might say, what ever we do as individuals will make no difference. We cannot change the world.

In some ways, business seems to be making serious attempts to put its own house in order, if not to change the world in which it operates. Long before recent scandals made headlines, the notion of Good Corporate Governance and Corporate Social Responsibility (CSR) were being promoted in boardrooms around the world. Sadly, this has not always been because it's the right thing to do, but because it's seen as being good for business.

In 1994, the Caux Round Table (CRT) published its Principles for Business as a guide to business practices in an era of globalization. The CRT recommends use of these Principles in all societies, whatever their religious and cultural traditions.

The CRT Principles call for business leaders to implement certain rules of corporate governance that include transparency, avoidance of corruption and favoritism, respect for the environment, and fair treatment of customers and employees.

Of course, there are many businesses that are run with integrity and honest intentions, guided perhaps by sincere personal beliefs. They do not seek to prosper at the expense of others and their management is genuinely concerned with creating benefits for the community at large. Wherever such businesses are, they are to be applauded, and encouraged.

We may not be able to change the world, but what we can do as individuals is to encourage honesty and integrity by our own conduct. The practice of honesty and truthfulness are basic principles in all religions, and at the very heart of Buddhism.

They can be seen, for example in the principle of Right Speech which urges avoidance of lies and deceptions, backbiting, idle talk, and abusive speech. The cultivation of honesty and truthfulness; to practice speech that is kind and benevolent. To let our words reflect our desire to help, not harm others.

Right Action tells us to practice selfless conduct that reflects the highest statement of the life we want to live, and to conduct ourselves in a manner that is peaceful, honest and pure, showing compassion for all beings.

Think for a moment what could happen if every individual in the world were to embrace those principles of honesty and truthfulness. Add compassion, a touch of tolerance, a dash of selflessness, a helping of loving kindness, and we have a recipe for true understanding.

Could conflict and strife between groups of individuals, between nations even, have any hope of surviving in such a world? I think not.

Telling it as it is

Euphemisms can obscure the truth and
should be treated with caution

These days, there seems to
be a whole new vocabulary for many practices that have
been going on for years. This seems especially so in
the world of business, and many of us who work in this
environment will be familiar enough with most of them.
"Human Resources," for example, which to me seems
a decidedly less than human description, is now used to
describe people.

Companies speak of their vision, of their corporate
objectives, their decision to focus on core competencies
consistent with the tenets of their strategic plan. They
remind us of their dedication to best practices, of their
unrelenting pursuit of excellence, of their commitment to

preservation of the environment. They are also mindful of the need to have in place comprehensive Risk Management and Crisis Management programs. Then there's Good Governance and Corporate Social Responsibility to which all Good Corporate Citizens must subscribe. Finally, they remind us that by continued attention to direct and indirect cost management, they will continue to offer customers a superior, value-added package of high-quality service at a competitive price.

This language of the business world and the more general euphemisms that have crept up on us, need to be treated with caution. They have been with us in all languages since language itself evolved, but recently their original purpose—that of softening reality, making it easier to accept—seems to have been taken over by a more sinister one of actually distorting it. And it's the business world again that has been quick to grasp the usefulness of the euphemism in downplaying problems. "Experiencing temporary cash-flow difficulties," has long been another way of saying we have no money.

Think for example, of that innocuous sounding phrase "collateral damage" that we hear so much about during military conflicts. Collateral, means something connected to, but aside from, the main subject, and damage means loss of something that is desirable. What collateral damage actually means in the military context is the supposedly justifiable killing of non-combatants in the interests of achieving a particular objective.

Let's take a few less sinister, but still worrying examples of contemporary usage. How about this one from the sensitive world of retailing. Know what shrinkage means? And it's not what happened to that silk shirt you put in the washing machine. Shrinkage is the word used to describe theft—shoplifting, that costs the retail industry a great deal of money each year.

Here's a few more. Drug addicts are called substance abusers, drunks are described as being inebriated, intoxicated, or tipsy. A brothel is called a massage parlor, pornographic shows are referred to as adult entertainment, and prostitutes described variously as bar-girls, hostesses, escorts, and masseuses.

A lie is a fib, a fabrication, a cover story, untruth, inaccuracy, and famously in politics, it has been a terminological inexactitude. When we're sick we're indisposed—and in the language of diplomacy, that's another lie, and if our children are noisy we probably describe them as boisterous youngsters. The neighbor's children are of course, always noisy brats. Short people are vertically challenged, and those that are fat, are described as generously proportioned.

Understandably perhaps, death itself seems to demand for many a kind of automatic euphemistic response. "How long has she been gone?" "Did she pass away peacefully?" Apart from passing away, some people simply expire or pass on.

Nowadays, as well as this tradition of avoiding "telling it as it is" there also seems to have developed a curious habit of making sure any charitable contribution to society receives the maximum publicity. Thus we see reports and photos of the managing director of this or that company against a background of the company's logo presenting an over-sized check to one deserving cause or another. Efforts such as these, by companies and business organizations to draw attention to their social contribution activities can often have the effect of provoking a perception of cynicism, and if ill-considered, can expose some such projects to ridicule.

In an annual report for instance, one international company, a global leader in its field, detailed its social contribution in various countries around the world. It spoke of its awareness of the annual flooding in one Asian country in particular, and the hardship and loss of life this brought to inhabitants of the region. "To counter the effects of this annual flooding and to help people at risk to better prepare themselves we have instigated a company-sponsored nationwide program of swimming lessons."

Yes, there it was in black and white, and if I remember correctly, underlined in red. One could just imagine the scene. As the hapless family watch their home and all their belongings being washed away in the raging flood waters they are consoled by the voice of the company representative who calls out from a passing boat, "Don't worry, you qualify for free swimming lessons under our nationwide program."

No doubt the management of most companies, although mindful of the publicity they may gain from their "social activities" are sincere enough in wishing to "give back to society," to help others. I just wish they would not see the need to draw attention to their efforts.

Telling it as it is in a world of self-praise, sanitized truth, and what is intended as social politeness, is not always easy. Fortunately, it's not always necessary either.

It would, for example, be heartless to say to an acquaintance, or even a close friend who's clearly becoming more obese by the day. "Wow, you're getting fatter and fatter. You must spend all your time eating." Far better to relate to the person with true loving kindness, making no mention of their obvious weight problem. Equally, when a colleague tells you her aunt has passed away you need only offer your condolences, no need to complicate matters by asking non-euphemistically, "When did she die?"

Right Thinking, and Right Speech, avoiding saying things that are hurtful or that might cause embarrassment to others, are mostly quite easy to put into practice. Basically it is simply a matter of saying less. If, for example, you don't smoke and someone offers you a cigarette you need only say, and perhaps with a slight smile, "No thank you." If you trot out the usual additional, "I don't smoke," you immediately risk being seen as offering an implied, and perhaps, self righteous criticism of smokers in general, and this one in particular.

Least said the better, especially if you're vertically challenged, and you're in a room full of very generously proportioned Sumo wrestlers.

Personality counts

Blending diverse outlooks may be a key to
happiness in work and at home

"She's such a happy person,
nothing seems to put her in a bad mood." "He's always like
that, always miserable, puts everyone in a bad mood—he
must have been born like that." "Oh, he's always fooling
around—never seems to take anything seriously."

When we hear comments such as these about people
we know, perhaps those we work with, we probably simply
accept that we're all different, that we all have a basic
personality. That's the way we are born, probably a genetic
thing we say, and we justify our reasoning with comments
such as, "She takes after her mother in that respect. Always
had a smile on her face, nothing seemed to bother her."

We certainly can't deny that we judge and categorize others in terms of their personality. This almost reflex mental action influences both our social and working lives. If, for instance, we're planning to invite a group of friends to our home for a relaxed get together, we will almost certainly take into account their various personality types when we're deciding who to invite, and try to achieve some sort of harmonious balance.

It's in the working environment however, that a person's personality really matters. It might seem obvious, but people are most happy at their work when doing something that best matches their personality. Acceptance of this fact by those in human resource management has not always been so.

Research over recent years, however, has shown that the link between a person's personality and the degree of satisfaction they derive from their work is clearly recognizable and can be predicted.

To try to place the whole idea of personality and job satisfaction on a scientific basis, psychologists established a set of five standard personality types that can be broadly described as:

Extroverts—sociable, talkative, friendly and outgoing
types
Introverts—quiet, shy, and retiring types
Conscientious—thorough, responsible, diligent
Emotionally Stable—agreeable, cooperative, caring,
trusting
Receptive to Ideas—creative, broad-minded,
insightful

Very interestingly, that same research has established
that of the five personality types, conscientious people
are more likely to perform their jobs efficiently over a
long period for a wide range of different types of work.
It gets even more interesting though, when we discover
that simply being conscientious will not help if you want to
excel say, as an artist or a musician. If this is where your
interests lie, you will certainly need to be the "Receptive
to Ideas" type with a little bit of the "Extrovert" thrown
in.

Choosing the kind of work we do, sometimes seems to
happen naturally. "I've always been fascinated by science
since my school days," says the university researcher.
"Farming just comes naturally to me, I guess it's in my
blood. I wouldn't do anything else," says another. There are
many other people however, who are attracted to particular

types of work that do not suit their personality, but which they pursue for a variety of reasons.

"All my friends work in advertising. It's well paid and you don't have to work too hard," says a trendy looking young person. "Well I don't really like having to dress formally every day, but my parents wanted me to have a proper job so I am working for a financial services company. I also have to study a lot. I can't say I enjoy it, but it's a job, and I have to think of the future," says another. Both honest enough comments, and both indicating a mismatch of jobs and personalities.

Understanding the importance of personality types can help both employers and employees to achieve that desirable state of a happy and productive working environment. Wise employers will take account of personality when interviewing or screening job applicants, no doubt placing a high level of importance on their assessment of a candidate's conscientiousness.

For their part, the sensible job-seeker will be aware of their own personality type and take this into account when applying for a particular type of job. "OK, the salary seems good and I could probably do the job if I put my mind to it, but could I really accept having to work away from home and all my friends? And with all the extra study, would I even have time for my music, and what about . . . ?"

Another interesting fact to emerge from the research into personality and its relationship with performance at work, is the degree to which a person's personality type can be used to assess their potential for leadership. We may not all wish to be leaders, but if our personality attributes include extroversion, emotional stability, and agreeableness, we can be described as having leadership qualities.

Although the importance of trying to match a person's personality and their type of work is clear enough, the psychologists and researchers may have overlooked another important factor—the opportunity for everyone of us to change.

We may well be born with a natural tendency to fit into to one of those five personality types, but by following the teachings of the Buddha, especially by practicing insightful meditation, we can achieve the inner peace and serenity that comes from understanding. And the joy that understanding can bring will be apparent to all. It will be very much part of our personality—how other people perceive us.

Our personality is, after all, the outward manifestation of our inner thoughts and feelings. It reflects our moods, our likes and dislikes, in effect what we are. It would not be reasonable, or desirable for everybody to have the same personality—one highly extroverted person in a small group is often enough. What is desirable though, is for all of us to recognize the importance of tolerance of the many personality types we encounter and often have to deal with on a daily basis.

One of the great joys of successful leadership is the reward of achieving harmony in a group of people with diverse personalities. And that harmony can only work for the common good.

The medium is the message

Buddhism teaches that in seeking the right
answers we must first ask the right questions

"The 24-hour news channel. We keep you up to date with the latest news from around the world 24 hours a day, every day." Breaking News, Business News, Sports News; it's all there, comprehensive, updated, in-depth coverage. This, as we are constantly reminded, is the Information Age, and to drive it, we have Information Technology. News is big business. The public's right to know has become the need to know.

The news that we apparently crave by the minute is brought to us by a variety of means that we refer to collectively as the media. Today, television of course dominates, both in terms of immediacy and worldwide coverage. If President George W. Bush stumbles, either literally or verbally, while delivering a speech, millions of people around the world will have viewed the event live via television or seen it repeated as part of that 24-hour news service. We can also catch it on the car radio, have it flashed at us from the Internet, sent as a message via our mobile phone and later of course, we can "read all about it" in the newspapers. "Bush blunders, Secret Service steps in."

Isn't this instant access to what's happening in the world something we should exploit to the full? Should we not feel privileged to be living in this Information Age in which we can watch a war taking place thousands of miles away unfold before our eyes? Certainly, we can marvel at the ever-developing technology that makes it possible, but before we become conditioned to seeing the suffering of others as yet another newsworthy event, should we not ask, why do we need to know?

Some of us will be familiar with the life's work and writings of Canadian Marshall McLuhan, a man considered by many to be a leading prophet of the electronic age. It was he in fact, who coined the word "media" and later the term "global village." His most well known statement, "The Medium is the Message," was a warning we ignore at our own peril.

Much of what McLuhan wrote was concerned with the effects of advertising and the way the media shapes our lives. News, like advertising, especially if it is manipulated, sends a message. It can strongly influence our views of a particular issue, stir our emotions, even cause us to embark on a specific course of action. Because today, news of every kind is also often instantly analyzed from every angle, with experts explaining technical aspects and others telling us how it is likely to affect future events, we can too easily lose the motivation to think for ourselves. It's a bit like instant noodles. Just add boiling water, no need to check the ingredients, we know they're good for us—it says so on the packet!

A basic tenet of the Buddha's teachings is that in seeking the right answers, we have first to ask the right questions. This is part of what mindfulness means; being aware of the information before us, taking the time to test its veracity, seeking to understand its message.

The news items that are fed to us by the hour and sometimes by the minute are simply snapshots of moments of time. They are there for their moment but we are always part of this moment. Think of how one event, the subject of intense media focus and debate, such as the contest for a major presidential election, quickly becomes a non-event once a new president is elected. How often did you flick through the pages of reports on a major military conflict in the daily newspapers, leaving them unread because the events they referred to had been overtaken by more recent ones? News quickly loses its appeal when we've heard it already.

Why should we have this craving for instant news gratification? Part of the answer, certainly with many young people, is our fascination with technology where the medium is indeed the message. If we know that simply by pressing a button on our mobile phone we can get the latest information on whatever interests us, it's something we feel impelled to do. Another reason is that we're constantly being reminded by the purveyors of news that we need to be informed about almost everything, with the implication that if we're not up to the minute, on top of the situation, somehow we are not fully equipped to function in today's world.

If a colleague at work suddenly says, "Have you heard the news?" And if we have not or don't know what the question refers to, we immediately start to wonder what has happened. Has the company suddenly gone bankrupt, the messenger won the lottery, the chairman's wife given birth to twins? An open-ended question like this is almost guaranteed to receive the response, "What news?" Our colleague is using that old trick of playing on our curiosity. Had the question been, "Have you heard that the messenger has won 10 million in the lottery?" Its effect would have been different.

It's obvious, and perhaps inevitable, that more and more, today's news is often managed, either by the media or by those who want to control or influence it. As the media increasingly becomes the message, it's more important than ever that we treat news and information with a questioning mind, prepared to see both sides of an issue, and not jump to conclusions.

Television in particular gives people almost instant access to any event. In doing so, it clearly diminishes, or destroys altogether, many of the close ties of family life that are based on oral communication. In its place, it provides a kind of global theater where people are actors on an electronic stage. It is on this stage that humanity can all too easily be reduced to yet another newsbyte; one which leaves little room for loving kindness and compassion before taking us over to the White House for an update on the latest events in Washington.

Older workers should be valued

Rising bias against old people is not justified
by research or common sense

The traditional respect that the young are required to show to their seniors has long been an integral part of many cultures. It is also inextricably linked with the core precepts of the Buddha and one that is universally admired.

Today, there are signs that, especially in the workplace, that those values which have guided successive generations of young people are being threatened by our technology-driven, and marketing-oriented consumer society in which traditional skills and values are seen by some young people as being outmoded and even irrelevant.

"I don't seem to be able to communicate with my children any more," lamented one mother recently. "They spend all their free time in front of the computer. wouldn't mind so much if they were doing something useful, but all they do is play games and communicate with strangers on one of those chat rooms. Even when their grandparents visit, they hardly notice their presence."

The need for young people to develop computer-driven communication skills is obvious enough in the business world where computer literacy is now essential for career development. Although this is to be encouraged, it must not be seen as an end in itself.

There will always be the perception by the young and ultra-fashionable that only they are in touch with what matters. They follow, and sometimes create, new trends in the way they dress and entertain themselves. This is nothing new; it's always been this way. Their perception that older people are not "with it" and will never understand them, is also another fact of the often discussed "generation gap."

The idea that older people are somehow less able to make a useful contribution in terms of performance is one that is shared by many young and not so young managers in business. Older workers are seen as less likely to adapt to new ways of doing things, especially tasks involving computer technology. They are also perceived as likely to be more frequently absent, less trainable, and less committed than their younger counterparts. Those who subscribe to this view often justify it with remarks such as, "You can't teach an old dog new tricks," and, "At a certain age people begin to lose their memory."

Although they may well still treat older people, especially the very elderly, with the traditional respect that is expected, and even demanded by most societies, they will still regard them as not being quite part of their world, not someone with whom they can fully interact.

That commonly held view is however, not only shortsighted; it is simply wrong. A whole body of scientific research has shown that on the contrary, older people at work are likely to be more committed, are receptive to new ideas, and less likely to be absent, than their younger counterparts. They are more committed for example because they have a strong sense of loyalty and responsibility, and are receptive to new ideas because experience has taught them that the development of wisdom requires an open and curious mind. They are also less likely to be absent than their younger counterparts.

As far as memory loss is concerned, research again shows that this generally happens only with people over the age of 65 who may begin to experience a slight deterioration in their short-term memory. Examples of sharp-minded and energetic individuals who pursue their interests or life's work when they're well past retirement age are everywhere. We all know or have heard of someone who fits into that category.

Computer games are one area where young people love to show off their considerable skills, often providing amazing displays of dexterity and problem solving, attributes in themselves which can only be admired, and which are clearly useful when applied to more serious tasks. When the latest hot games product is launched it's likely to attract a keen and knowledgeable audience of these savvy youngsters who exchange comments and remarks in the verbal shorthand only they comprehend.

True to form, when one new and much awaited game was launched recently at a computer show, there was a large gathering of these young gamesters milling around the stand, eager to discover what features the new game promised. Sample versions had been made ready, and were available for customers to try out on a number of the specially prepared play stations. Among the jostling crowd, an old man with thick-lensed glasses and a walking stick was seen peering at one of the computer screens. Very deliberately he tapped the keyboard and moved the mouse carefully, smiling quietly when the monitor displayed a sudden burst of super realistic animation. "Just look at him," one youngster whispered to his friends, "Do you think we ought to show him how it's done?"

Their half joking discussion was interrupted by an announcement from the small group of company officials. "Ladies and gentlemen, before we reveal to you the amazing features of one of the most exciting computer games available today I would like to introduce the man whose groundbreaking and innovative technology has made them possible. One of the foremost leaders in games technology and designer of . . ." Making his way to the microphone amidst a burst of applause from the obviously appreciative audience, was the old man the youngsters had thought might have benefited from their help.

This topical story illustrates a curious contradiction of how we regard and value older people. We readily accept that in many areas of education and professional disciplines, those from whom we learn and seek advice such as teachers and doctors will often be in the "old people" category. We know too, the maturity and wisdom they acquire from simply experiencing life can be invaluable sources of inspiration and guidance of benefit to everyone. Yet, in the context of the workplace, or in areas considered the preserve of the young, the value and the contribution older workers can make to the success of any business enterprise is often overlooked.

Simply accepting the fact of growing old, even tolerating older people with a sort of benevolent compassion, is not enough. We must appreciate that, although they are simply further along the path of life, they share the same moment with all of us.

And if they have the wisdom to live it with joy, wonder, and an ever questing and questioning mind, we can only benefit from their presence.

Agreeing to disagree

To deal with conflict, we must first recognize
it and identify its causes

When we think of conflict
we tend to think of a situation where there is strong
disagreement, even hostility, between individuals or groups
of people. Of course it manifests itself at every level,
between governments and the people they represent,
between one nation and another, between groups of
nations. We all know that when this happens, war, with its
inevitable consequences, can follow.

As individuals, we may not be able to do much to influence
conflict between nations. Whatever our views, most of
us can only watch as the opposing sides become more
entrenched in their positions and the diplomatic language
becomes more openly antagonistic and combative.

Conflict in our daily lives however, especially when it arises at work, is a different matter. This is something we can all do something about. First, we can consciously seek to prevent it and when eventually it raises its unwelcome head, as one day it surely will, we can, with love and understanding, resolve it.

Have you ever gone to work in an optimistic frame of mind, keen to get on with the project at hand, only to find your usually friendly and enthusiastic colleagues looking morose and sullen? Something is clearly wrong. Perhaps the problem lies with something you have said or done, or it may be related to something or someone else. You sense conflict may already have occurred, or that it is brewing, and while you are aware of the situation and do not wish to say or do anything to make it worse, you naturally want to know what's going on.

Recognizing that conflict exists, is of course, the first step in resolving it, and in doing so, we often believe we know what causes it, especially when it happens in the work environment. "It's all a matter of poor communication we say, "How can they agree on anything when they hardly talk to one another?" "Our manager never explains anything properly. How can he expect us to do what he wants?" These, and similar comments are common enough when something does go wrong, but are poor communications really the main culprit? In fact, research shows that while not communicating properly can be a contributing factor to work conflicts, problems more often occur from personality clashes and organizational problems.

Personality clashes tend to flare up between people when the underlying differences in people's attitudes, characters, and feelings that are normally kept in check, become polarized by a particular event, which challenges an individual's fundamental thinking.

One member of a project team for instance may advocate a "get tough" method with a supplier to get a particular job done on time—demanding that deadlines be kept whatever the cost, while another member of the team may feel strongly that a more understanding approach is not only more reasonable, but more likely to get results. Such fundamental differences can quickly lead to a confrontational situation and the seeds of conflict, with others taking sides, are sown.

Conflicts resulting from organizational problems occur because different departments have different priorities. When for example, bonus-related production targets are threatened by quality control demands, potential for conflict is high.

How we handle these work-related conflicts can make all the difference between what can be the beginning of a long-running feud, or the opportunity to quickly resolve potential problems, and clear the air on important issues.

Clearly, each conflict situation demands its own approach, but there are well-proven general rules that we ignore at our peril. There is, for example a natural tendency, particularly in some non-western cultures to downplay the situation. Managers may try to ignore the obvious signs of trouble with a breezy, "OK, let's move on folks." It's important in this context for those of us with managerial responsibility to realize that people with strong opposing views look to us to recognize and identify the nature of a problem and to take the initiative to try to settle the ensuing dispute in a fair, and even-handed manner.

The good news here, is that there are approaches that work, and perhaps the most effective is the direct approach. This uses the tried and tested techniques of problem-solving where the opposing views are recognized, discussed, and analyzed in a joint and balanced effort to assess the merits of each with a conclusion being reached based on consensus and goodwill. It is generally successful, because it leaves everyone with a sense of resolution; issues are brought to the surface, and dealt with.

Another technique, the bargaining approach, works when both parties have ideas on a solution but cannot find common ground. The focus is on finding a compromise. There is a price however, because compromise is just that, it involves give and take and no one may be completely satisfied.

The "OK let's look at the problem, discuss the merits of both points of view, then I'll make the decision because I'm the boss," method will work in the sense that the problem gets resolved, but it is one that should only be used when neither of the first two approaches results in a solution. It is likely that the person whose views are overridden may harbor resentment, and for the sake of future harmony may have to be continually appeased.

Finally, conflict can sometimes be resolved by an appeal to the good sense of those involved. "It's really not worth arguing about, and certainly not worth jeopardizing our normally friendly, and cooperative working relationships. After all, we are all trying to achieve the same ends. We need simply to agree how we should do just that."

When conflict arises between people, it is often seen as a negative force, one that promotes ill feeling, anger, and resentment. It can however, trigger a natural process of cleansing and healing.

To deal with conflict we must first recognize it and identify its causes. In doing so we will look deep within ourselves where the seeds of anger and intolerance lie dormant. When these are exposed to the pure light of Dharma, they cannot survive.

When we disagree with others, even firmly, yet do so in a spirit of loving kindness, tolerance, and compassion, conflict becomes consensus, even when we agree to disagree.

True colors

First impressions count, but they can also be
very misleading

The young man was in his early
twenties, and his mother noticed he had been getting ready
for another evening out with his girlfriend for most of the
afternoon. This was in marked contrast to the usual, "'Bye
Mom, we're going out to eat with some friends, won't
be late back, see you later." On those occasions, "getting
ready" meant a quick shower, a change from one set of
casual clothes to another, a check of the fashionable "Fido
Dido" hairstyle, and perhaps a few gulps of fruit juice.

All that was left to be done was to muster a cheeky
reassuring smile and he was gone, leaving Mom to shake
her head in bemused resignation.

This day though, was different. When he finally emerged, maternal resignation turned into wide-eyed amazement. Now "de-spiked," his hair was sleeked back, giving him a mature, conservative look and together with the neat shirt and tie and well-pressed trousers, he looked like everybody's idea of a smart, well-dressed young man.

Trying to adjust to this remarkable transformation, Mom naturally wanted to know where her remodelled son was going. "Oh, Jane's introducing me to her parents for the first time." And then flashing that trademark cheeky smile, he added, "Got to create a good first impression."

The idea that first impressions count is one we've heard since childhood, and like the young man about to meet his possible future in-laws, we tend to take it seriously and generally make a special effort to present ourselves in the best possible light when we're likely to be judged by others.

Although scientific research confirms that first impressions do indeed count we need to remind ourselves that this process works both ways. Whenever we meet someone for the first time, just as we are forming that all important initial impression, consciously or not, they too, are evaluating us. In fact that same research demonstrated that an initial impression, based on appearance and demeanor, is created in the first 60 seconds and when we start speaking to one another, a final impression is formed based on what is said during the next 45 to 60 minutes.

Perhaps though, the most important result of this research, is that once that first impression is formed, neither party changes their opinion quickly or easily.

The part played by Right Thinking, Right Speech, and Right Action in this introductory process can be clearly seen when we learn also that in those first few minutes, impressions are formed by body language (70 percent), tone of voice (20 percent) and what we say (10 percent).

First impressions then, play a vital role in how we relate to one another and because of this, especially when we are judging other people, we need to look beyond the attractive physical appearance and the pleasing words. People trying to impress others, especially in a job interview will often present themselves in a way which they believe will suit a particular situation. Often too, those strong first impressions can be way off the mark, and a rush to judgment can lead to problems later on.

Consider also, the fact that in most relationships between married couples for instance, initial impressions formed under the heady mixture of romance and lust tend to change, sometimes dramatically, over time. Ordinary friendships too, are often broken when one person sees the other in an entirely different light.

The folly of relying on first impressions is brought into sharp focus when formerly respected public figures for example, are caught out betraying a scandalous and hitherto unrevealed aspect of their character. We may have seen them on television or even met them personally, and in that "first impression moment" believed what they said and were favorably impressed by how they said it, because that's what we wanted to hear.

We were taken in by the pleasing physical appearance, the carefully judged body language, the well-chosen words and the gentle, modulated voice.

When we see the real character of such people exposed, we find it hard to accept. "I just can't believe it," is a common reaction on these occasions.

How we judge other people in those initial moments when we meet them for the first time will depend largely on our own values. The most successful journalists and professional television interviewers know that by being open, non-judgmental, and by asking questions in a relaxed, conversational style, they can encourage the person being interviewed to "open-up," often revealing heartfelt emotions that would be difficult to fake. People who respond to one another in this way very quickly do so because a sense of mutual trust is firmly established in those "first impression" moments.

Whether we are dressed in our best, "meet the public" attire or wearing our favorite lolling around the house clothes, the impression we convey to others when meeting them for the first time can always be the same if we demonstrate tolerance, understanding, respect, and humility. If we are open and straightforward with everybody with whom we come in contact, their immediate impression of us will be based on what we truly are. In that same spirit, their response will also more accurately reflect their true nature.

Presenting ourselves as we are is especially important at work when we are likely to encounter "first impression" situations on a regular basis.

If physical appearance, enhanced by expensive clothes is important to us, then those factors will clearly influence our initial assessment. If we are wise to take the time to base our judgment on less superficial factors we will discover the true nature of persons we work with or meet in a business environment and with whom we must establish a relationship based on mutual trust and respect.

By the way, what were your first impressions when you began to read this chapter of *Dharma Moments*? If they were favorable you will have continued reading to this point, demonstrating yet again, that the more we are impressed with what we see at first glance, the more we will want to know.

Dharma moments in daily life

The road to nowhere

Compassion and understanding can
overcome fear, anger, and envy

Remember those first gnawing
pains of childhood toothache? "Just forget about it and it
will go away," we might have been told by well-meaning
friends or even parents. Of course the pain didn't go away,
although when we became occupied it might have faded,
but it was still there, and eventually the bad tooth that was
the cause of it all had to come out.

Isn't this what many of us do even as adults when
something unpleasant or worrying occurs in our lives? We
try to forget about it, hoping it will go away. And the more
we try to ignore it, the worse it becomes.

It's the same with our emotions, especially those negative feelings and responses such as anger, fear, and jealousy. We have all experienced them and most of us still do, how we deal with them though, makes all the difference. Let's take a closer look. We'll start with anger.

"Don't get mad, get even." Most of us have heard that slick comment but we know that's not the answer. The first thing we must do is to drop the "get even," bit, then we're half way there.

In Buddhism, anger is classified as an unskillful state of mind. This is very important, and it is crucial to see that there are no exceptions. Buddhism allows no place for "righteous anger." In other words, there is no conceivable case where anger is justifiable or where it is the most appropriate response.

This might be hard to accept. It is easy to think of numerous examples of real grievances and injustices that would seem to justify anger. But whatever the situation, an angry response is not smart. When we're angry, we cannot think clearly and we may well say or do something we will later regret. Whichever way we look at it, getting angry will only make the situation worse.

Being mindful of anger is the first step. Think of it as a poison. Applying the antidote of loving kindness is the next step.

If you are driving on the expressway and some aggressive driver cuts you off, you have a choice. You can allow your anger to flare up, flash your lights, rant and rave, or immediately cut it off with a thought of loving kindness, "I hope he gets home to his family safely." Try it, it works.

Can we do the same with fear? Well, like anger, we must recognize it for what it is—a physical and emotional anxiety about something known or unknown, over which we have no control. And often, it's the unknown which causes us the greatest fear.

Fear is always within ourselves, it's there only because we allow it to overcome our rational thought. Being mindful of fear in all its forms will allow us to deal with this very basic emotion without which many creatures would not survive. Think of the classic "fear, fright, and flight" reaction of animals, including humans, and which in our case, can cause us to jump out of the path of sudden danger. But fear can often be destructive unless we tackle it head on. And when we do, the fears we have nursed, and which have caused us so much anxiety, often turn out to be groundless.

Let's take a simple example. Your boss at work is especially keen on "team spirit," he expects everyone to play their part and has little time for "shirkers." He's planned a big charity event for a weekend that clashes with your close friend's wedding. You want to tell him you can't make it, but are scared of his reaction. You feel that not taking part might even affect your chances of promotion. You consider making up an excuse after the event, but that would mean lying. As preparations for the charity get under way, you feel trapped. Your "fear factor" increases dramatically.

Finally, you overcome your fear and tell him about having to attend your friend's wedding. "That's wonderful," he says, "I love weddings and wish I could be there with you, but as you know we have this charity event to take care off. I remember meeting your friend at that sports day last year; please give her my best wishes."

Even in situations where our fears are justified, allowing fear itself to take over will only make a bad situation worse. Staying calm and thinking rationally will often save the day.

Applying this approach to dealing with jealousy may seem to be completely unworkable. Jealousy, and its close ally, envy, can be even more difficult to conquer than anger or fear, both of which are usually short-lived. But jealousy and envy can exist for as long as we permit them and while they do, they can be especially destructive.

The first thing we must accept about jealousy and envy is that they lead nowhere. Being envious of someone else's achievements or possessions will not bring them to us. In fact, while we harbor these negative emotions, we are less able to get on with our own lives. Our situation is likely to get worse, creating a negative cycle of events. So how do we deal with the emotion, often described as a "green-eyed monster." The answer again, is simply loving kindness.

By substituting loving kindness for envy, when, for example, we hear of another's success, we can feel joy on their behalf. When a loved one gives us cause to feel hurt, left out—jealous in fact, we can, in a spirit of loving kindness, know that we have no cause to fear if our love is true. Anger, fear, jealousy are there only with our permission. Replace them with loving kindness, compassion, and understanding, and they simply will not exist.

Beyond sight and sound

The evidence of the impermanence of our material world is there for all to see; the only constant is change itself

There's a very old dog in the compound where friends of mine live. Their house is fairly old and set in a corner and looks on to trees and greenery that is home to birds, squirrels, and the occasional cat. "We really love it here," they say, almost every time I pay them a visit. "We know we're in the city, but this little bit of nature is so relaxing, even inspiring."

Most days, the old dog too, makes its rounds of the garden. It's completely blind and deaf, but it seems to have retained its sense of smell which it uses like an olfactory radar as it shuffles and bumps around.

When I first saw this old family pet I wondered why it had not been put to sleep by the owners. Surely, I thought, it would be kinder, more humane.

On a recent visit one of the owners, a family doctor, was in the garden and as I looked compassionately at the glazed eyes of the old dog, he seemed to anticipate my question. "We decided we have no right to end its life— you know it's strange, but in its own way it copes very well. It recognizes all the familiar smells and seems almost content in its own world."

As we spoke, the handicapped animal lumbered slowly to its feet, and as we watched it shuffle away, its nose close to the ground like a bloodhound, I tried to imagine how I would cope with being both blind and deaf. The more I thought about it, the more horrific it seemed.

Imagine it for yourself. First, the complete darkness, that only the blind can know, then the total absence of sound that produces a silence that is more than silence.

I sat down on one of the wrought iron garden seats near my friend's house. The afternoon sunlight dappled through the trees and two squirrels performed their arboreal acrobatics, and there was the twittering and tweeting of birds. I could see and hear, at least with my eyes and ears.

There in the distance was the dog, tired perhaps from its rounds, it appeared to be sleeping in its favorite shady spot. Was it dreaming I wondered? And if it was, could it see and hear in its dreams just as we do when we enter that mysterious and colorful realm where sounds and sights are all around us, but where our eyes are closed in sleep, and our ears deaf to the outside world?

The 19th century American poet, Henry David Thoreau wrote, "I hear beyond the range of sound. I see beyond the verge of sight. I see, smell, taste, hear, feel that everlasting something to which we are all allied at once."

Isn't that how we see when we practice mindfulness? In particular when we practice meditation? At first we are blind, then we learn to see with an ever-increasing clarity. We are deaf, but as we progress with our meditation we learn to hear the very whisperings of the mind.

Suddenly I viewed the dog with great respect. The doctor was right, it did seem content with its lot, and seemed to know its place in the order of things. And it was a perfect example of mindfulness. An inspiration to me to be more mindful. By using its remaining senses of touch and smell it was able to navigate its world, a world whose smells and textures change constantly, stimulating the old dog to follow its exploring instincts. To live yet, in spite of the darkness and the silence.

When we are blessed with the health and vitality of youth we are usually also not yet wise enough to understand that it will not last for ever. Not even for more than a few years. In our folly, we tend to believe that we are the exception. We will never end up like the old dog, and even if we ever did, we would rather die, we say, than live like that.

Well, now we know better. The evidence of the impermanence of our material world is for all to see, from our own ever-fading youth, to the once familiar icons of our world, being no more. Nothing stays the same. The only constant is change itself.

A few days after my visit, thoughts of the old dog came back into my mind as I was busy in my office. A phone call, then an e-mail to deal with, but I let the thoughts stay, and then, in a quiet moment, I visualized the sniffing, shuffling animal as it made its way around the garden. I also recalled the trees and the greenery, the leaping squirrels and sounds of the birds, and wished I had the power to let the dog see and hear again.

Meanwhile, I resolved to be yet more mindful. Mindful of the world we see and cannot hear, of which we hear, and cannot see.

Nothing is what it seems

Viewing the world as an illusion can be a
surprisingly powerful means to discover
the true and joyful nature of the Dharma in
ourselves

When I was studying abroad, I
lived for a while in my own apartment, and perhaps in the
folly of youth, decided to brighten up my bathroom. Chose
a yellow color for the walls—in fact I remember the label
on the can, "Sunshine Yellow."

I set about my task with enthusiasm, imagining how
my little bathroom would look with its new coat of paint,
and wishing I was more skillful as a painter and decorator.
Fortunately, I had carefully laid old newspapers to catch the
inevitable drips, and as I progressed, learning not to load

the brush with too much paint, I was able put most of the "Sunshine Yellow" on the walls.

Finally, late in the afternoon, the job was done. My hands were a mess, the brush looked like a yellow lollipop, but the newspapers had done their job, and as I cleaned up I sang my own version of that lovely whimsical Beatles' hit, "Yellow Submarine." "We all splash in our yellow bath-a-room, yellow bath-a-room, yellow bath-a-room . . ."

Pleased with my efforts, and my choice of "Sunshine Yellow" I surveyed my work with youthful pride, and right on cue, the sun beamed through the frosted glass of the window. Time to get on with my studies, I told myself, I could not live in the bathroom, however bright and cheerful it was. And then, to my dismay I spotted two large blobs of yellow paint on the bathtub. It was made from the newly fashionable acrylic, plastic-like material, and I knew removing the yellow smears without damaging the surface, would be difficult. I would have to be very careful. I could not use any type of solvent. Hot water, perhaps that would do the trick.

A few minutes later I tried this approach using a rag dipped in a bowl of hot soapy water. With small circular movements I tackled the first spot. No effect. If anything, the paint seemed to have been absorbed into the surface of the acrylic material, and appeared even to be increasing in size after my efforts with the hot cloth.

I began to be anxious. My rental agreement with the landlord stipulated that I would be held responsible for any damage to furnishing and fittings, and I could hardly afford to pay for a new bathtub. I decided to seek advice, and called a fellow student who was majoring in industrial chemistry, perhaps he could come up with something that would work. His comments though, were not encouraging. "If the paint has been absorbed into the outer surface of the bathtub, anything you do to try to remove it will only make it worse," he said, adding, "why don't you paint the whole tub yellow." I told him that wasn't funny, and decided to put it out of my mind and went to close the bathroom door as a sort of symbolic gesture.

The sun no longer shone through the window but the yellow walls had certainly transformed my "bath-a-room." What a pity about the bathtub I thought. If only I had covered it completely I sighed, glancing once more at those offending yellow stains, and turned to close the door.

I paused and took another look. Where were they? Could no longer see those yellow marks. I peered closely. They had completely disappeared. Just then the sun cast a late afternoon beam through the glass, this time the light dappled on the floor, spotting the dark tiles with yellow blobs of fading sunlight. Yes, I had actually been trying to remove spots of light from the bathtub! How could I have been so foolish? They must have moved slightly even while I was desperately trying to remove them. And I didn't even notice.

Of course, when I related all this to my friends it caused much merriment and mirth, especially when the sun shone through classroom windows. But later in life, as I learned more and more about Buddhism, it also became an important lesson in the illusory nature of what we may believe is real.

Is this material and physical world the true reality? Or is it all an illusion? Does it exist only in our minds? A young novice monk, observing a flag blowing in the wind asked a fellow monk, "Is it the wind that moves the flag, or the flag that moves the wind?"

The answer, that it was the wind blowing on the flag that caused it to move, seemed obvious. But the young monk was not satisfied, he saw it in a different context and believed that the moving flag must, in turn, influence the wind. They turned to the abbot for an answer. "It is neither. Mind is moving," he said.

Understanding that reality exists only in what we refer to as the mind—which itself is simply a means of communicating with a greater cosmic consciousness—is a first step towards true contentment.

As we strive to loosen the bonds of desire and the unhappiness they inevitably bring, the acceptance of the physical world as an illusion allows us to become truly fearless and relaxed in our life. We can accept things and people as they are, or as they seem to be. We can take life as it comes, finding something of value in everything, even in suffering itself.

One of the subjects I took as a student was art, and especially after my yellow bathroom experience, I soon realized that reality—color, for example, disappears as light fades. All shapes and colors being products of light, thus appear to vanish with the onset of night. Then there are the many tricks used in drawing and painting that rely upon creating an illusion of dimension and texture, and even of light and shadow.

Eventually I asked myself, "How is reality any different from a dream. And if it is not possible to perceive any substantial difference between the two, why bother to believe there is a difference?"

Viewing the world from this standpoint, that it is an illusion, can be a surprisingly powerful means to discover the true and joyful nature of the Dharma in ourselves.

We know that whatever color we paint our walls, it is only there in our mind's eye.

Just like that lovely Yellow Submarine.

Animal virtues

All living creatures deserve our loving
kindness and compassion

I am not a great watcher of
television. I find most of the programs neither entertaining
nor interesting, and while like most of us, I feel the need
to keep up with the news, these days I brace myself each
time I turn to the news channel, fearing yet another report
of a tragic event.

There are however, certain programs which do get my
appreciative attention. Often beautifully and skillfully filmed,
they can have all the poignancy of a great tragic drama,
the fascination of an unravelling mystery thriller, or provide
the inspiration of a heroic tale. I have watched births that
take place under the most amazing circumstances and
precarious conditions. I have witnessed battles between

tenacious adversaries. And I have seen some of the extraordinary strategies and methods evolved by living creatures and plants to ensure their continuing survival.

Yes, it's those wonderful wildlife programs I'm enthusing about, although I sometimes think if I see that same cheetah chasing, and finally catching, that poor Thomson gazelle one more time, I too will take off at "more than 70 miles per hour!"

And I am not in favor of what seems to be a recent trend for humans to get in on the act. I really do not want to see hands-on "experts" wrestling with crocodiles or a wannabe Doctor Doolittle tickling a tarantula. It's the other living creatures that fascinate and inspire me. Give me the quiet narrative of a genuine naturalist and let the animals, insects, birds, and fish, speak for them.

And who, you may ask is sounding like Dr. Doolittle now?

For me, the natural world is one great symphony of birth, life, death, and rebirth. A world whose myriad creatures in their infinite variety have evolved to play their specialized part in an ever-evolving, interdependent system. And it is a world where these same creatures display what can only be described as virtue.

It has been said by a leading professor of natural history that animals may not be ethical, but they are often virtuous. Can animals actually display virtue? We must accept that ethical behavior as defined in the Five Precepts is solely attributable to human beings, but in the higher animals at least, there are so many examples of virtuous behavior that we must also accept its existence.

We have all heard of, and perhaps experienced, the acts of domestic animals, especially those by "Man's Best Friend," the family dog, that can have been motivated only by a sense of virtue. I recall reading even of a wild monkey in India that jumped into a river to rescue a human baby. Was this an instinctive maternal act? Did the animal mistake the human child as one of its own offspring? Whatever the cause or motivation, the act itself was undoubtedly virtuous.

We are constantly being reminded by scientists that we meddle in the natural world at our peril. Sadly, when we do, the wildlife also suffers, driven sometimes into extinction by the excesses and self-serving interests of humans. I was particularly saddened when one of the wildlife programs recently included images of racks of elephant tusks. In many Asian countries the elephant is an integral part of our cultural heritage. Yet, we can all see the sad sight of these great beasts being used in our cities as a means to generate income for their human caretakers. We remind ourselves that from the mighty elephant to the tiny ant, all living creatures deserve our loving kindness and compassion. All of the higher animals can distinguish between a non-caring attitude and kindness, between compassion and cruelty.

We know of course that by their genetically determined nature which is programmed to ensure their survival, animals, especially those we refer to as wild, can be rapacious and apparently cruel. They literally devour their prey, sometimes in a sickening and horrific manner until they too fall victim to a bigger and even more voracious hunter. Such is the way of the natural world.

From the Buddhist point of view, this apparently cruel and abhorrent behavior is understood, and its purpose— that of ensuring survival, is also accepted as being part of the cycle of life and death. As Buddhists we do not ask "Why did God create all those obnoxious and dangerous and disease-spreading animals?" The flies that pester us out of doors and sometimes even inside our homes. The bloodsucking mosquitoes and the cockroaches to be found almost everywhere. They are all part of the same world as the cute kitten, the faithful family dog, and the noble horse.

If we then accept that animals can be virtuous, does this also mean that although they have no sense of morality, or even the need for it, that they can be subject to karma?

The answer must surely be that because Buddhism sees all life from the perspective of infinity, the cycle of birth and rebirth has always existed. The karmic record of every living being extends also into infinity and each has a potential of karma, both good and bad. Because of their lack of moral values, animals can be said to be subjected to karma passively—in the same way, for example as mentally retarded humans.

I was discussing this question of Buddhism and animals recently with an American friend who lives here with her family and who follows Buddhist principles. After a fairly serious and at times weighty discussion, she recalled a story about one of her friends—let's call her Liz—who worked in a pet store.

Animals such as mice are recognized as being "feeder animals." Pets have to be fed and while some eat "pet food" others eat other animals. And this is where mice come in. They are feeder animals and sometimes sold as such by pet stores.

Liz liked almost everything about working in the pet store except when she had to sell mice as feeders. But Liz was a smart lady and she quickly found a true Buddhist solution.

Whenever anyone wanted to buy the mice, she would ask if they were for pets or feeders. If the person answered feeder, she would chant a Buddhist mantra three times to the mice so they could have a better life next time.

One day, a customer came in and bought some mice from another assistant who had taken over from Liz during her break. Seeing the customer about to pay for them, Liz asked. "Excuse me, are they for pets or feeders?" "Feeders," answered the customer, adding, "and please don't be chanting over them, the last three I bought that were chanted over got away!"

The sound of silence

When we see or hear things as they really
are, acceptance comes naturally

The negative side of the ubiqui-
tous cellphone, perhaps the most intrusive innovation of
today's technology-dominated world, was brought to my
attention one day in a well-written and clearly heartfelt plea
by a columnist in a national newspaper. And recently, in the
same newspaper there was a bitter condemnation of the
excessive level of noise caused by a night market near the
city's most popular park.

Just two of the long list of thoughtless, and plainly
selfish acts of some people. We can all add to this list,
the street vendors obstructing the footpaths with their
carts and stalls, the motorcycle taxis monopolizing the
pavements and sellers of all kinds, loudly advertising their

products. All creating inconvenience to others—and often, excessive noise.

Apart from complaining, as individuals there's little we can do. Noise is all pervasive in cities and this seems especially so in our capitals. Shopping malls, those great caverns of cacophony, assault our ears with a deluge of decibels, department stores, even government offices and banks, all contribute to this most distracting and even debilitating form of pollution.

In one branch of a major bank that I use frequently, and I must admit, increasingly reluctantly, a high-volume television competes with the radio for the customers' attention.

Noise then, as it affects those close to it, can certainly be regarded as a form of suffering—an example of the First Noble Truth and our need to be free from its torment, as a form of craving as described by the Second Noble Truth.

At this point, it's logical to ask, if we have no control over it, how can we be free from the noise, thus achieving the state of the Third Noble Truth—the cessation of suffering? I recall asking a similar question to one of my *Vipassana* meditation teachers when I first discovered the life-changing potential of insight meditation.

The small meditation center was housed in a sort of garden pavilion on the grounds of a large old house that had so far defied the then high-rise building boom. Sadly, at the time of my weekly visits, construction on an adjacent site was often in full swing. A far cry from the conditions one would expect for anyone wishing to meditate.

Seeing my pained expression, when, on my very first visit the noise from the site burst in with a vengeance, almost as if it was designed to deter us from our purpose, the teacher asked what I thought was an odd question. "Does it bother you? The noise, does it upset you? Does it spoil your concentration?"

"Yes, it does. I find it most disturbing. It's also annoying. It's beginning to make me angry. After all don't we need a quiet place in which to concentrate?"

"Yes but the quiet place is within us. The noise which you find so distracting is external. It only exists if you want it to."

My expression now was one of puzzlement and seeing that his answer did not satisfy me, especially as the crashing and banging continued unabated, the teacher motioned to our small group to gather around.

"If we approach meditation from a selfish point of view with the ambition to achieve perfect silence, all noise will become our enemy. When we think like that, we become very emotional, and then where is our meditation? If we notice that we are becoming short-tempered, we should know that we are meditating in a wrong way. Never allow yourself to meditate like that!"

"Noise is a challenge. If we can make it part of our meditation, we will make real progress. If can do this, we will feel confident that we can literally meditate in the middle of the traffic. Noise will no longer bother us."

He explained further, "While meditating, some people get disturbed by what they see . . ." As if to dramatize the point, a dazzlingly bright light from a crane on the building site swung across our vision.

Allowing himself a slight smile, the teacher continued, "they close their eyes in order not to see what is in front of them, but then something else will start disturbing them. Meditation should not be an excuse to blame something or somebody for taking away our inner peace.

If we accept everything that comes our way, nothing can bother us any more, and our inner peace is there all the time. The point is that whatever obstacle arises as we meditate, if we blame that for our not finding inner peace, then eventually every object becomes our enemy."

The teacher continued, "Once when I began a long retreat, I had a comfortable house next to the monastery. Everything was perfect for practice. A few weeks after I arrived however, the monastery decided to start a major building project right next to my house. The whole area became a building site, full of heavy machinery, so my whole house was shaking. I felt that my retreat was ruined. It gave me so much trouble I could hardly meditate. I finally complained to my teacher, and he said something that really helped me. The noise, he said, is your meditation. 'You must make it your friend.'"

"How can we do that?" I asked. "Right now I feel irritated. In fact, I'm trying to eliminate the noise from my consciousness, but I can't."

"To begin with, you have to see suffering in its entirety before you can see your way out of it. Right now, you have a craving for the workers to stop. There is already aversion in your mind. Suppose you were in the midst of doing something that was very important to you. This aversion might flare up into anger, hatred, or even violence. Aversion is already a stressful state. Anger, hatred and violence bring on even greater stress and suffering, both to oneself and to others. These are the truths that we have to face every moment of our daily lives. But we are not aware of this aversion and suffering, we are in an unwakened state (*avija*). We blame our suffering on someone, or something else."

Smilingly gently, the teacher then asked me to think about the noise that was annoying me in a calm manner. Still smiling, he asked "What happens to the annoyance?"

"When I become aware of the annoyance, it sort of lessens."

"As soon as you become aware of the annoyance, the aversion fades away. It resolves in the mind. Is it still there?"

"You mean the annoyance? It's much less. It is still there but it is much less now."

It was true. Simply by thinking of it in this way the noise had faded, and with it, my annoyance. I realized it's not a question of putting the irritation out of our mind. It is a question of accepting the fact that we are irritated and annoyed. The issue was not the noise; it was my reaction to it.

We can see that it is possible to break the cycle of suffering by merely looking into our own state of mind, by being mindful in the truest sense. The act of mindfulness is a transcending act. It transcends likes and dislikes, and purifies our vision. We see things as they are. When we see or hear things as they really are, acceptance comes naturally.

A powerful force for change

Integrating loving kindness and compassion
into our everyday lives

A Western visitor to a Thai temple, the author of many books on cuisine from around the world, took the opportunity to ask an elderly monk a question on the relative merits of the world's cuisine from a Buddhist perspective, "Tell me," she asked, "of all the world's many dishes, which do you think is the most delicious?" "That which is served with loving kindness," smiled the monk. A lesson for the food writer and for each one of us.

Food of course can be both for the body and the mind, but however nutritious it may be, if it is offered begrudgingly or in an unpleasant, negative atmosphere, we will not find it appealing, and either not accept it or do so in sufferance.

Hand in hand with loving kindness, is compassion. Just as the mind and body are interdependent, so too these most basic of human qualities are intertwined, and immensely significant. They should form the very core of our thinking, of how we behave towards others, of how we regard ourselves.

But all the loving kindness, and all the compassion in the world will do little to help others unless we integrate these qualities into our daily lives. Merely paying lip service to the notion of "doing good" by occasional and often very public acts of charity, will do nothing to benefit others or ourselves. These very positive qualities, although gentle and loving in nature, are in fact, a powerful force for change. Anger and vengeful thoughts and actions can melt under their influence. Hatred itself can turn to love, envy to respect.

A distraught young girl once sought the advice of the wise old man of the village. "Please, you must help me," she said. "My grandmother is such a wicked woman. She seems to hate me and does everything to make my life miserable. She seems jealous because I am not old and wrinkled like her and can still dance and sing. I try to please her, but nothing I do makes any difference. I cannot stand it any longer. If she died I would not be unhappy."

"Well it seems she is resentful of your youth and beauty. Her attitude will only get worse so I will give you this special lotion. It is very powerful but you must apply it gradually," counseled the old man. "After a time changes will take place, your oppressor will be gone and your troubles will be over," he added, and patted the girl on the shoulder. "Go on, take it, but remember you have to rub it in slowly, and do it every day."

Although at first the girl had no thoughts of doing anything so drastic as slowly poisoning her tormentor she had become desperate, and accepted the lotion from the old man.

The very next day, pretending to show concern for her grandmother's aches and pains, she persuaded the old lady to let her massage her, gently rubbing in the secret lotion. Knowing she had to be patient, the girl put up with the sarcasm and ungratefulness of the old lady and persevered with the daily massage sessions.

One day, to her surprise when the lotion was down to the last few drops, her grandmother took her hand. "You know my dear, you are not such a bad girl. I think I have misjudged you. After all you are my granddaughter. Let's start again, I think we can be friends, don't you?"

Responding in tears to this sudden change of heart, the girl realized she did not want to lose her grandmother after all and raced back to the old man. "You must do something quickly. I did what you told me, but she changed, and well, now we love each other and I don't want to lose her. You must give me something to save her." He took her hands in his and smiled a knowing, old man, smile: "You have already saved her by your act of loving kindness. Your tormentor has gone, as I said she would, and your troubles are over."

To be able to put loving kindness and compassion into practice as a living expression of Dharma we must first love ourselves. With loving kindness within, we can transcend anger and hatred, which cannot coexist with gentleness and compassion.

How often these days, do we become consumed with anger by what we perceive as somebody's unacceptable behavior?

We may not be able to change the world, but with loving kindness and compassion we can dissipate our anger and in the spirit and practice of Dharma, begin to understand the human condition.

Lazy excuses

Reaping the mental, physical, and spiritual
rewards of a job well done

"Do not deceive yourself with
laziness, which thinks to practice tomorrow or the next
day, or you will die praying for help. Quickly, quickly help
yourself and take the essence of truth." (*His Holiness the
7th Dalai Lama—Songs of Spiritual Change.*)

Most of us will admit that some of the time, we are
guilty of that tempting vice of laziness. Often it's in the
form of putting off a job that needs doing, from say, the
morning, to the afternoon. Then we tell ourselves we'll do
it after dinner. Spurred by guilt, we make another attempt
to tackle it, but by now we feel too sleepy, and the task
remains unfinished.

His Holiness the 14th Dalai Lama describes three types of laziness, each easy to recognize, and each of which most of us are guilty. They are the laziness of indolence, leading to procrastination described above, the laziness of inferiority—doubting your abilities. "I could never learn to do that, I'm just no good with computers." And the third type of laziness, often seen in young people today, the laziness of attachment to negative actions—mindless pleasures as seen in the obsessive interest in computer games.

I sometimes encounter what I call pre-emptive laziness from friends or colleagues when I ask for example, "Are you going anywhere near the Post Office on your travels?" "I'm afraid not, I'll be tied up all morning." Believing I am about to ask them some favor which might involve them in a minor inconvenience, they immediately pre-empt any further questions such as "Would you mind posting this letter for me—it's already stamped?"

These days becoming overweight, for many people around the world, is a major problem, and children are not exempt. Recent estimates, widely published in the press, show that in the majority of "developed" countries around 20 per cent of children of school age are overweight.

Yes, they eat too much of the wrong type of food, but according to the research, a major reason for their being overweight is their lack of physical exercise and their preference for lolling around watching television or playing computer games.

The type of laziness which can lead to overweight and all the associated medical problems is particularly insidious. The more we shun exercise, the fatter and lazier we become—it's a self-perpetuating cycle of cause and effect.

When we are feeling particularly lazy, we probably ask ourselves, "So what's wrong with my taking it easy for a change? I've worked hard all week. I reckon I deserve a break, why shouldn't I put my feet up?" The answer is clear enough of course, and it's in the question. If we really are simply taking a well-deserved break we would not be prompted by guilt to justify our laziness in disguise, even to ourselves.

We probably know there's some outstanding job we must finish. Our well-deserved break is simply yet another excuse for procrastination. We must finish the job first to earn that "well-deserved break."

Recognizing laziness is one thing. But how do we avoid it? How do we break that self-perpetuating grip on our lives?

In practicing mindfulness we think about every aspect of our being and of the world around us. And in confronting laziness, indolence, and sloth, we also practice mindfulness. We can do it in carrying out the most simple everyday household tasks to the more complicated routines of our workaday life. Whatever the task is, we must approach it in a mindful way, remembering everything we do is of the moment and resolve to do it methodically and thoroughly and not to be diverted by sensual distractions.

If it's a report we are trying to finish before lunchtime, then we must do our best to finish it. If it's something that requires a great deal of effort on our part to do well and the sacrifice of our leisure time, then we must make the effort and sacrifice our leisure.

Does this mean that we have to be "workaholics" not to be lazy? To devote ourselves to our work with no regard to leisure time? We all know that fortunately, it is not the case.

What we may not fully realize however, is that by not being lazy in every sense of the word will bring enormous benefits to ourselves and to the lives of others.

On a very practical level our bodies will benefit from the effort of walking instead of taking the car to the local shop, of cleaning out the spare room this week-end instead of at some indefinite time in the future.

Mentally we will be free of that gnawing guilt that never lets up. And spiritually we will have taken an important step along the path of Dharma.

Lessons in humility

Only by being truly humble can we achieve
the perfection we seek in life

The more ripe a cluster of rice becomes on a growing rice plant, the lower it bows down its head.

As we progress through the many stages of our lives, many of us believe that becoming good, in the sense of being virtuous, kind and considerate to others, honest and open in our relationships, forgiving and tolerant of the perceived transgressions of others, charitable to those less fortunate than us, at least in the material sense—is our ultimate goal in life. But we must learn that achieving all those virtues that we believe constitute goodness is not enough. Our ultimate goal in this life must be to become humble. Only then can we achieve the greatest happiness and joy.

Becoming truly humble, as we all know, seems sometimes almost impossible. In our daily lives we are confronted with situations where we believe our skills and knowledge are superior to those of the people around us. We watch them struggle with a particular task and feel we want to take over and show them how it's done. But there's always something they can do better than we can, and when that happens, it's our turn to be humble.

Some years ago, in the early 1930s, a young European girl, a talented musician and a budding concert pianist was visiting Bonn, Germany, the quiet university town and birthplace of Ludwig van Beethoven. Naturally, Beethoven's house, by then a well-preserved museum, was to be the highlight of her visit. Accustomed to the admiration of her peers and the praise of music critics in her own country, she felt somehow superior to the other visitors who like her, were being shepherded around the house.

And suddenly there it was. A piano, once used by Beethoven, still gleaming in its polished beauty with its lid open as if waiting for the master to create his musical magic. She could not resist. She sat on the padded stool, and with a quiet confidence, began to play a short but well-known piece. A burst of subdued applause from the other visitors greeted her impromptu performance. Feigning modesty, with phrases such as "Well, I do play a little in my own country," she was thrilled with the reaction. Her feeling of superiority now felt even more justified.

Just then a slightly frail, elderly man had quietly come in to the room and he too was now seated at the piano. But he simply sat there, almost as if in meditation.

Another visitor in the group came over and whispered in her ear. "Do you know who that old man is?" She had no idea, and shook her head. "That's Paderewski, the Polish pianist, probably one of the greatest in the world today."

Hardly able to control her excitement, the girl watched as the old man still sat quietly at the piano, saying and doing nothing. She decided she had at least to take the opportunity to speak to such a world famous pianist. But when, she wondered, would he begin to play? Finally she approached him.

"Mr. Paderewski, aren't you going to play?"

"No, young lady, I am not going to play. In fact I am not worthy to play on this piano. I can only respect it."

"I am sorry Mr. Paderewski, I don't understand."

The old man turned, admonishing her with his eyes, "This, young lady, is the piano of Beethoven, my teacher. I am nothing before this piano, before my teacher, I am totally worthless. I am not worthy even to touch it." When she listened to his words, she was deeply moved. It was the beginning of her own humility.

The girl was at the growing, the developing stage of her life. She had respect for Beethoven, a great composer and pianist of the past and no doubt for the prodigious talent and mastery of the great Paderewski, but she was not humble before their presence, daring to play on the piano that once was played by Beethoven himself and expecting Paderewski to do the same.

In the other sense of being good, being accomplished at what we do, our work, a sport or hobby, we thrive on the admiration of others. We like to show off our talents, often at the expense of those less gifted. In this sense too, being good is not good enough. We must know the limitations, pettiness, and emptiness of our being. We must become humble in all that we think, all that we speak, all that we do.

If we are truly bowing our heads before the Dharma, that is itself our liberation. The perfection that we seek in our lives is already there, we need only to be truly humble to achieve it.

Window on the park

Don't let your judgment be clouded by selfish
desires that can obscure loving kindness

It was late on a Friday evening.
Sam had been working hard all week, and he was tired,
both mentally and physically. Even at this late hour the
traffic on the expressway was still heavy, and now it began
to rain. A few heavy splashes at first that did not quite
seem to demand the services of the windscreen wiper.
Then suddenly it came in a great rush.

Sam turned the wipers on full speed, but even then it
was difficult to see ahead and he slowed down, straining
his eyes through the dancing torrent to make out the lights
of the other vehicles. And then came the thud as his pick-
up was hit from the rear. He heard the crunch of metal

against metal and felt a terrible pressure on his chest, and then all was blackness.

When he next opened his eyes he could see only the white ceiling of the hospital room. His seatbelt had saved his life, but he had suffered severe injuries. He was able to speak and hear, and even see, but for many weeks he would be immobilized, unable to turn his ahead more than a fraction either way.

Soon, with the aid of a mirror, he was able to take stock of his surroundings and realized the voice that had introduced itself as Robert was that of his roommate, an elderly man who had been crushed by a heavy load in the factory where he worked. He too was quite ill but as people do in such situations, they soon began to talk to one another whenever possible.

One day, Robert, whose bed was next to the only window in the small room they shared, was able to sit up for the first time. Starved of the signs and sights of the outside world Sam was excited at the new possibility of knowing through his fellow patient something of what was happening beyond their four walls.

With the limited movement of his right hand he was able to adjust the mirror and see Robert propped up on his pillows. "What can you see, what can you see now?" he demanded excitedly. "I can hear children's voices."

"Oh there's a beautiful park down there, right next to the hospital. There's a pond. Children are sailing little boats. And there's a dog that's just jumped in the water after a stick . . ."

"What else, can you see beyond the pond? Come on, please tell me more."

And so it was that everyday when Robert was allowed to sit up he would describe to Sam what he could see through the window. It came to be the high point of their day and even when Robert seemed tired, Sam badgered him to know what was going on outside.

One day, as Robert was being propped up by the nurse, it began to rain. They could hear it pattering at first on the roofs outside, then thudding with the roar and force of a downpour. Just as suddenly it stopped, and Sam as usual was eager maintain his connection with what he believed was the real world—his world that had been so cruelly and unfairly wrenched from him.

"So what's going on in the park now. Is there anybody there? The nurse had been about to leave but now she looked quizzically at Sam, then to Robert who had twisted his head to the window that was parallel with his bed.

She paused for a moment, then walked over to the older man and straightened his wispy hair gently with her fingers, then, smiling silently to herself, she quietly left the room.

That day, Robert described the park as it slowly shook off the rain and once more welcomed the warming rays of the sun. How people began to appear on the still wet paths. How the sun once more danced on the water and children reappeared, playing along the water's edge.

Sam ached to see this all for himself and knew if he were by the window he could position his mirror for a perfect view, and anyway, perhaps soon he too would be able to sit up.

He thought more and more about this. Why should the old man have the best position? Why should he have to rely on him for a second-hand commentary when he could see for himself if his bed were close to the window?

As the days went by he became more and more resentful and began to lose interest in the daily descriptions from Robert, who, far from improving, seemed to be getting weaker judging from his voice and the long silent periods when he appeared to be asleep.

Just as he had hoped, the doctors told Sam that in a few days he would be able to sit up, and if things went well, they might even be able to remove the brace from his neck that had kept him almost immobile. But he was warned, there would be weeks, possibly months ahead of being confined to his hospital bed. Having that window position became even more important to Sam, and in his selfish obsession, Robert became an obstacle to his goal.

That very night he was awakened by the noise of violent coughing. The light was dim but with a practiced twist of his mirror he could see Robert slumped half out of bed, his body jerking with each cough. Sam reached for the button that would summon the nurse, and then stopped, letting it slip from his hand as the body of the old man slid almost in slow motion on to the cold tiles of the floor. When Sam finally pressed the call button it was almost dawn, and Robert's lifeless body was removed as if it were nothing more than a bundle of soiled sheets.

It seemed certain now that Sam would get his wish. "Of course we'll move you by the window this afternoon. This morning we'll get you sitting up without your head brace," said the nurse, adding, "I expect you will miss Robert, you really came to rely on him didn't you? You know, he had a very kind heart as I am sure you will soon realize."

Puzzled slightly by the nurse's last remark, Sam occupied himself with the anticipation of his new freedom, quickly dismissing any thoughts of his former roommate.

Finally, about the same time as when he would listen to Robert's halting yet compelling descriptions of the park and all the comings and goings that so enlivened his day, he was wheeled to his coveted position by the window. And now he could even turn his head. The warm afternoon sun had already brightened the window frame and Sam, slowly, almost breathlessly twisted his head to catch the view that Robert had so often described.

The sign on the gray wall opposite said "Parking" and all around were the gray bare walls of the hospital car park.

How often do we allow our judgment to be clouded by selfish desires? Desires that can obscure loving kindness. Desires that can twist our thinking until we become so obsessed with satisfying them that others are seen merely as an obstacle to be removed.

Desires that eventually will bring us up against a blank wall.

WINDOW ON THE PARK

It's never too late

Unacceptable behavior by others must not
intrude on our inner silence

Two reports in the weekly
entertainment section of my newspaper caught my eye.
The first concerned a heartwarming account of how veteran
film actor Tony Curtis, now 78 years old, was appearing in a
stage version of the classic musical "Some Like it Hot" in
which he first starred more than 40 years ago.

Why heartwarming? Well apart from the great photo
that showed the actor in a reassuringly relaxed and familiar
pose which to me said, "If he can do it, so can anyone," the
story of his struggle and final success in overcoming both
alcohol and drug addiction and his reappearance at this
time of his life in an active stage role, all that is extremely
heartwarming.

It is also a lesson in the dangers we all face in this increasingly liberal society. Describing how he had succumbed to some of these dangers, Tony Curtis talked of how the breaking point for him came in 1981. "I wasn't happy with my marriages, I wasn't happy with the films I was getting. The next thing I know, I'm using cocaine and alcohol, and the next thing I know, I'm immersed in it."

It's a familiar story, especially for those individuals showered with fame and fortune. In the case of this particular star he recognized the danger, and did something about it.

Referring to his young sons from a previous marriage he recounted how he wrote himself a letter, "If you want to see these boys grow up, you'd better take control of yourself." He did just that, and went to Hawaii for five years. There he spent his time painting. "I didn't need people."

Today, not only does he appear to have achieved contentment, both in his personal and professional life, according to the article, he also seems to be a thoroughly nice person with a real sense of humility. Whenever he sees someone in a wheelchair, says the writer, he kneels down, offers his hand and says, "Hi, I'm Tony, who are you?"

The other report, on the same page was about another actor, Kevin Kline. The essence of the story was how the actor seemed to identify with a character he plays in one of his more recent films, an old-fashioned prep-school professor.

A key point in the film illustrates how the highly principled teacher in a battle of wills with a rebellious student finally gives in to human frailty and bends his own principles. Commenting on this, Kevin Kline, says, "Hundert (the teacher) doesn't live up to his own principles. He gives in to human frailty. I think we can all relate to that. What he eventually sees is the seduction of our culture by the well-packaged person or idea."

And referring to the student named Sedgewick he adds, "It's the prevalent rationalization that the end justifies the means. That's what drives Sedgewick—he wants to win, and he doesn't care what it takes."

That last comment gave me much pause for thought. It seemed to highlight much of what causes disharmony in our society today. A craving for success or recognition of one kind or another, a lack of loving kindness, intolerance of the views and needs of others, dishonesty, and a complete lack of humility.

Speaking of what he sees of the attitude of youngsters today, the actor said, "A lot of kids just want to work as little as possible, and make the most money possible. There's no love of learning, of acquiring knowledge and wisdom, of understanding history or current events. They don't know what's going on in the world. They want to kick back and play with their computers and watch TV."

Kevin Kline was no doubt referring to American children, but he could well have been talking about youngsters in most countries around the world. Certainly many parents could identify with his sentiments.

In the competitive world of business, this behavior is all too common. We encounter it in the work environment, often almost daily. We may wonder sometimes what we're doing wrong.

The rudeness, arrogance, or plain mean-minded attitude of a colleague or boss can have a devastating effect on everybody around them. They seem to be intent only on achieving their own ambitions, not caring who they trample on in the process.

So, how do we deal with this kind of problem, of the behavior of those who "want to win and don't care what it takes." This survival of the fittest philosophy, now being made even more fashionable by television programs that seem to glorify "winning" at any cost?

First we must recognize it is the problem of the individual who behaves that way. Unacceptable behavior by others of any kind is just that. It should not, and must not, intrude into our inner silence. It must not cause even a ripple on the surface of our pool of calmness and serenity. It exists only if we admit it.

We can also see that to thrive, "bad behavior" requires an audience, a target for it barbs, for its sneers and put-downs. We must also remember that people who are consistently unpleasant to others are often battling their own fears and demons. "I don't mean to be like this. I just can't help it," they will say. Others will justify their actions by claiming they cannot afford to show "weakness" by being kind or considerate to others. They live in fear of themselves.

A little girl, constantly rejected by her father when she tried to climb on his lap for much needed affection, finally asked her mother tearfully, "Mommy, why does Daddy hate me so much." Taking the child in her arms, the mother explained, "He doesn't hate you dear, he's just scared of loving you."

There were many lessons in these two articles, with the comments of Kevin Kline reminding us that the "end justifies the means" mentality is also reflected in politics and in the world of business. And his lament that children seem only to want to "kick back and play with their computers and watch TV," certainly strikes a chord.

It was though, the image of veteran actor and entertainer Tony Curtis, smiling almost exuberantly in his stage costume, that reminded me so graphically that by looking within ourselves, we can indeed find happiness and contentment.

Changing times

The natural inclination to cling to the past is
a road to nowhere

"The party's over, it's time to wake up." Those half-remembered lines of a once popular song take on a new meaning when at the end of one series of twelve months we look forward, perhaps with some uncertainty and even trepidation to yet another New Year. Another? Well, new years do have a habit of coming around with monotonous regularity, and in spite of all the revelry that marks the annual passing of the old and the advent of the new, their very persistence can be an unwelcome reminder of the relentless passage of time.

As we get older our perspectives inevitably change, and as each new year comes and goes we have to make adjustments. The cozy world of our youth no longer exists.

Familiar icons, stars of the entertainment world for instance have been growing old like the rest of us but we haven't given it much thought and when suddenly we see them as they are today, well, it can be quite a shock.

Sometimes if the person was a special favorite of ours we feel somehow let down. "How can anybody change so much, I can't believe it's the same person," we say when perhaps we see one of our favorite stars in a television interview. We forget of course that we too have changed. And when we are confronted head on with that unwelcome fact, we are reluctant to accept it.

Have you ever looked at contemporary photographs of yourself and felt almost embarrassed at how unattractive and old you look? Years later you come across those same photographs and just can't help almost saying out aloud, "Wow, is that me? I can't believe I looked so young. I looked great." Friends who see the photos tend, of course, to put us in our place with comments such as, "Yes, so what happened?"

It does seem to be a fact of human nature that however much we may be aware of the impermanence of all things, of the cycle of birth, life and inevitable death, we seem to want to believe that as an individual, we are different. As teenagers, perhaps after a visit to our grandparents, we might well have said "I'm never going to be old. I couldn't bear to look like that."

The Buddha reminded us of the five fundamental truths of existence that cannot be challenged and that apply to every one of us:

1. Growing old is a natural condition. There is no way to escape it.

2. Suffering ill-health is a natural condition. There is no way to escape it.

3. Death is a natural condition. There is no way to escape death.

4. Everything and everyone changes; we must part even from loved ones.

5. My thoughts and my actions are my only true belongings. I cannot escape the consequences of my actions. My actions are the ground on which I stand.

Just as there is no escape from these fundamental truths, there is also no escape from the absolute necessity of their acceptance. Growing old can be described as the

Dharma of all composite things. And when we fully accept that eternal truth, our fears of growing old, of becoming ill, of losing loved ones, and of our inevitable death, will no longer lead us in futile attempts to change the nature of things.

Recently, I watched with a kind of bemused fascination a television program illustrating the extreme lengths many people, especially those in the entertainment business, will go to in their vain attempts at staying young. Actually when you think about it, the expression "staying young" is both a contradiction, and an impossibility.

That of course, does not deter the diehards. They subject themselves to the surgeon's scalpel, to injections of a toxin that effectively paralyses their facial muscles, they endure all manner of abrasive and other treatments and mostly they do it in secret. "My face is my fortune," they say, but they fail to grasp another very basic truth—other people simply don't care. In fact, most of us when confronted by someone who is just too good to be true will find it makes us uncomfortable and difficult to accept that individual as a person.

For men, perhaps the most common example of age denial are the attempts by the balding to first experiment with every type of remedy and then, when the inevitable happens, to resort to the always obvious toupee. Instead of enhancing the wearer's appearance, the artificial hairpiece is more often a distraction.

This was vividly illustrated in the follow-up to the film classic *The Magnificent Seven* which starred the charismatic and shaven-headed actor Yul Brynner. In the inevitable sequel the original cast was replaced, and Yul Brynner's action role taken by a middle-aged actor with a hairpiece. Needless to say, the film was less than successful with the star being remembered only for his comical appearance.

The natural inclination to cling to the past, though understandable, is literally a road to nowhere. Far, far better then to follow the wisdom of the Buddha. To accept that we will indeed grow old, and that the physical world around us also constantly changes.

We can all see dramatic evidence of changes that have taken place in our life time, both in the world at large, and in the world we have touched and which has been part of our environment.

Think back just a few years for example to a city that you knew then—one without high-rise buildings, with no shopping malls and entertainment complexes. And to a world without television, without computers and the all-pervasive Internet.

It has been said that the only constant of change is change itself. It might also be said that for many of us, accepting change and growing old gracefully is one of life's greatest challenges. The freedom we achieve by overcoming it, can also be one of life's greatest joys.

Defeating depression

The despair we feel at the occurrence of
destructive events in the world around us
can be cleansing

"How are you today?" "Actually
I'm feeling a bit depressed. I don't know why really.
Everything seems so pointless. It all seems to be a waste
of time, and I seem to have no energy for anything." At
some point we will all have heard a similar answer to the
"How are you?" question. We may well have given such an
answer ourselves instead of responding with the expected
"I'm fine thanks."

However resolute and positive we are, one day we
wake up to a world that seems overwhelmingly, well—
depressing. International conflicts and natural disasters

compete for our attention with a host of unending tales of local corruption and its consequences. Everywhere man's inhumanity to man is reported, often in horrifying detail.

We see and read reports of the changing weather patterns triggered by our unrelenting pollution of the environment. Of flooding, caused by destruction of forests, of wildlife threatened with extinction, of natural resources over-exploited for short-term gain. Enough examples, we say, to fill a book. Indeed many have been written that highlight these dangers and what appears to be a whole "Green" industry has developed over recent years, dedicated to countering these destructive and polluting forces.

Isn't all this enough to make anyone feel depressed? After all, if what we perceive as the state of the world did not affect us, what would that say for us as individuals?

Being depressed though, is different from suffering from what nowadays is described as depression, a condition recognized by doctors, yet still not fully understood from a psychiatric point of view. Depression is a state of extreme unhappiness, described by some sufferers as a black, dismal, dungeon of despair; as a stifling hot room with no means of escape; as a heavy overcoat of pain, and like walking through molasses.

It can be precipitated by many factors, but from the Buddhist perspective however, the main cause of depression can be described in one word—selfishness, satisfying our own needs and pleasures above those of everyone else. The "me first" attitude, whether it's pushing to the front of the line, making sure we get the best food first, the best seat at the show, the most praise for something we do in competition with others.

"Wait a minute," you say, "being selfish may not be a good thing, but how can it lead to depression?" There are two main reasons. The first is that unhappiness arising from selfishness is cumulative. When we do not get what we want, or are stopped from doing what we want, we often over-react to a ridiculous extent. How many arguments at home or at work have arisen from quite petty causes related to being selfish? Such behavior naturally isolates us from others, and as this pattern of behavior is repeated, our self-confidence is eroded.

Self-obsession smothers consideration for the needs of others and we stop giving love. Our preoccupation with satisfying our own desire to be happy blinds us to the needs of our family and friends, and we do nothing to help them. And because we no longer receive their love in return or the simple and pure joy of making them happy, the cycle of isolation continues. We sink further into unhappiness, self-doubt, and even thoughts that we are going insane. This is depression.

What can we do to break this depression cycle? First we must recognize that the despair and despondency we experience as a reaction to the negative and destructive events in the world around us can, in themselves, be a cleansing act. In the practice of Dharma we will encounter negative karmas as we face up to the suffering we must all experience in this world. When we wash a dirty piece of cloth for example, the water becomes black with dirt. We don't see the black dirt as a negative thing since it means the cloth is getting clean. So, in this sense, when we get depressed at this level, we should perhaps rejoice.

To tackle what the medical world calls clinical depression, we clearly need to look deep within ourselves to rid ourselves of the concept of "I." Think about it; without the ego to nourish it, depression cannot exist.

We can also help ourselves in very practical ways. Every morning, when we wake up, we face a new day. How we make use of that precious time is entirely up to us. Why not start the day with a smile? A friend of mine says each morning as he's brushing his teeth he tries to recall an amusing incident or story from the day before. When he starts laughing he knows it's time for his shower.

Apparently his early morning laughter routine is infectious and when he comes down for breakfast, the rest of his family demand to be let in on the joke.

That's the great thing about a cheerful disposition, and its close companion, a sense of humor—they're catching, and there are very few places or occasions where they're out of place. Most public speakers are well aware of the value of humor in putting their audience at ease, and some are wise enough to use it as a means to bring cheer and comfort to others.

My own high point of unintentional humor came when, as a student I was asked to repeat that well-known remark of Britain's Queen Victoria, "We are not amused." I knew it was something to do with humor, but I just couldn't remember the exact words. Finally, I thought I'd got it. "Don't make me laugh," I said triumphantly. And since then, I can never think of that period of British history without laughing.

Wherever I go, there I am not

The familiar face triggers memories and an
instant desire to catch up on news and we
open with that familiar battery of questions.

"Oh my goodness—how are
you? It must be months, more than a year, what have you
been up to, and Tony and the children?" You bump into an
old friend, almost literally while out shopping. The familiar
face triggers memories and an instant desire to catch up on
news and you open with that familiar battery of questions.
"Are you still working at the same place? And your mother,
how is she these days?

"Yes, I'm still working for the same company I . . ." Before
your friend can finish you place a hand on her shoulder then
lift it gently in a gesture that you have something to say that
just can't wait. "Oh I must just tell you, we've had the house

completely redecorated. Well more than just redecorated. Remember the last time you came over and Tony had such trouble trying to park the car, almost got stuck between that big old tree and the wall? Well it's gone completely."

You pause just a fraction to catch your breath and for the ambiguity of what you've said to register—to make way for your very small joke. This is the friend who always could be relied on to smile on cue, the perfect ego flatterer. Even the smallest and silliest pun would cause her face to beam, then stay sort of half-illuminated as if waiting for another one—perhaps the really big joke, one that she could retell and bask in the second-hand glory of the mirth it would create.

"Gone completely, the tree, not the wall. What a difference it's made. So much more space and there's much more daylight in the house. Best thing though, there's no more parking by ear." You watch her face waiting for the inevitable question, "Parking by ear, what do you mean?" But it doesn't come, just a puzzled, almost faraway look. Never mind she has to stand there and listen dutifully while you get your silly little joke in. After all she is a good old friend and that's what good old, reliable friends do. They listen and they smile, and laugh as appropriate, even when they've got much better things to do.

"Parking by ear, PBE—you know a bump here, a bang there. And no whistles by the way. Whistles are absolutely against the rules of PBE. So you can tell Tony, next time you come over, he can park right outside the front door on the first try. How is he by the way, still spending half of his time at the golf club?"

It's a busy time of the weekend and the shopping mall is crowded. You and your friend have been gradually jostled into the garishly lit doorway of a music shop. "Love is in the Air," says a life-size display proclaiming the release of a new "romantic" album.

"Tony, he . . . he died about eight months ago. On the golf course actually, the doctors said it was a heart attack."

The flashing lights from the display inside the store paint your friend's face in intermittent shades of blue and red, and you're not even sure if she's crying. You want to say sorry for your self-obsessed prattle, sorry for not picking up the clues earlier, sorry for pressing on with your nonsense, so intent on getting your silly half a joke in that you gave her no opportunity to say what she wanted.

You really want to say sorry, but it is your friend who apologizes.

"I'm sorry, I should have called you when it happened but it was all such a shock. I thought the only way I could cope was to pretend nothing had happened so I kept it all strictly in the family and those who already knew or would have to know. Most of the time everything seemed so unreal. Even now every time I hear a car pull up outside the house I half think it might be Tony coming home from work or more likely from his golf."

"Oh, I'm sorry too. I haven't given you time to get a word in." You reach out and take her hand. "Let's go and get a coffee."

The first lesson here is obvious enough, and it drives home the truth of the old saying. "I hear what you're saying, but I'm not listening." The second lesson is perhaps less obvious, but it gets right to the heart of the problem, and tells us why we're not listening. It is simply that in the situation with the two friends, one at least was not living in the moment.

I was discussing this problem recently with an American friend who lives and works in Thailand. He had just begun his own journey of discovering the Buddha's teachings and his insightful comments were revealing.

"This has been the story of my life, with my eyes fixed on the past or the future, or an eye on each but with no attention paid to this particular moment. Yet this is all life truly is: a succession of particular moments. What a shame it is to miss them! I'm washing dishes and worrying about getting the taxes done or the bills paid. I'm driving the car and worrying about something I screwed up at work. I'm trying to fall asleep and I'm dwelling on something I said to my wife or child or friend that didn't come out right.

"Too often I go through life being inattentive, taking everything for granted; a loving wife, wonderful, healthy kids, the beautiful countryside as close by as a window permits. It is so hard to be fully present in the moment. What a waste! This moment is the only one I can do anything about, but I'm not here. Wherever I go, there I am not. Too often my life is like a play in which the leading actor hasn't shown up—and there's no understudy ready to jump in."

"Wherever I go, there I am not." I found that phrase especially graphic. For me it perfectly describes the state of not being mindful of the moment, whether that moment is one of sadness or joy, pain or pleasure, boredom or exhilaration.

But my friend then described how he has put the teachings of the Buddha into practice.

"One Friday night I practiced mindfulness with my children. After watching a movie, we lay around on the family room floor for an hour or more talking, sharing stories, and arm-wrestling. For once I was not thinking of something else or trying to do two things at once. I was there, and they were there, and we connected in a deep and a fun way. This was what I call practical mindfulness."

Let's remind ourselves that the term "Buddha" means the Awakened One. More than anything else, this means being awake to and fully conscious of, this moment. Each of us can be a Buddha for at least this moment.

All we have to do is be aware. All we have to do is be here, now.

Special relativity

Dharma vision places everything in
perspective

It was a hot afternoon and the
water sprinkler was arcing its spurting jets across a thirsty
patch of grass in the garden.

A black and white finch hopped in and out of the free
shower as a cat watched from the shade, too lazy to follow
its instincts and chase after the bird. But a squirrel high up
in the dark, gray-green folds of the mango tree was as agile
as ever. One moment poised on a branch, highlighted by
a shaft of sunlight, the next it was gone, startled perhaps
by my incautious approach. From branch to branch, tree to
tree—then in one mighty leap, to the eaves of the house.

I settled down on a seat in the shade thinking about how I fitted into to all this. I looked around and took note of the overwhelming presence of green, and then marveled at the many different shades of that most basic of nature's colors. The light, almost translucent yellowy green of the banana fronds; the olive green of the leaves of the mature mango tree and the myriad variegated greens of the plants and shrubbery, all set against the backdrop of the green of the grass.

I watched as an ant crawled over the back of my hand, realizing that the indentations of my skin and the ridges created by my veins would, from the ant's perspective seem like part of a rather barren landscape. Was that tiny creature aware, I wondered, that it was scurrying over part of another living and breathing creature, albeit of somewhat larger proportions? In fact, do ants and similar small creatures have any real sense that we humans exist?

The little bird, refreshed perhaps, had flown off in a sudden swift flight to a high point on a neighboring house and the cat, stirred by this departure, stretched and padded off in search of new distractions. I was left with my thoughts and the ant, which by now was negotiating the patterned holes in the white top of the cast-iron garden table.

So, how do we humans fit into the world of the bird, the squirrel, the cat, and the ant? Probably, from their point of view, just as part of the landscape. Each of them lives in a different universe of sizes and shapes, sounds, sights, and smells. The small finch enjoying its garden shower has a life-span of from perhaps five to fifteen years; its hearing is much more acute than ours; it sees in color and can see ultraviolet light—oh yes, and it can fly.

The "garden" squirrel can't fly, but it can move faster in a tree than it can on the ground, and if you've seen a squirrel in tree-hopping mode, you will know that's very fast. It can also fall around thirty meters without getting hurt—it uses its tail as a sort of parachute. It probably sees only in black and white, and has a life-span similar to that of the finch with which it shares its territory.

And the ant? We're told it lives on average about five years, but it's difficult to imagine how the world must appear to this tiny insect. Although it sees in color, it appears to hear and communicate very selectively using a kind of vibration system. This means when it's trapped underground it can send out a message to the Ant Rescue Service, but is oblivious to the noise generated by humans. So no use shouting at it to go away, better to learn ant talk.

I had been sitting there for quite some time, musing about the different worlds and dimensions occupied by the creatures I had seen. The light now was beginning to change. Soon it would be that dream time so beloved by photographers; soft mellow tones, slowly fading hues as the day wound down. Whose world is it anyway? Isn't it yours and mine? After all, what would an ant know about photography, or the finch and the squirrel for that matter?

The answer is that the world as we experience it belongs to the moment, whether seen through the sharp eyes of a bird, the black and white vision of a squirrel or the-still-to-be-understood senses of the ant. It's obvious enough that animals, birds, and insects will perceive "our world" differently from one another and from us.

But do we overlook how we too, you and I, also see things differently from one another?

Once, on a trip to a forest with some friends, an older member of our group just stood gazing from our viewpoint at the panorama of the distant hills and the forest canopy below. We all paused, wondering what had caught his eye. All we could see were a mass of treetops and the vague shapes of the faraway hills. "I used to come here as a kid," he said. "Over there, there used to be a stream. The water was so fresh you could drink it." We smiled and nodded, understanding a little more about our own perceptions of the world in which we are just fleeting visitors.

Accepting that every one of us experiences the world differently, allows us to truly understand the feelings and sensitivities of others. But to do this takes more than just a sort of passive acknowledgement that we are indeed all different. We must make that extra effort to see the world through the eyes of all those we come in contact with. We must practice a special kind of empathy; we must see and listen to the world through Dharma Vision and Dharma Hearing. With the understanding and insight that comes from Dharma wisdom, also comes compassion and loving kindness.

Before I left the garden, a truly magnificent butterfly fluttered onto a nearby flowering shrub. Yet another view of the world. How long, I wondered, does a butterfly live? I looked it up. On average, about one month. To the butterfly, a lifetime. To you and me, a few chance encounters in the garden.

The perils of procrastination

Life's problems, once tackled head-on and
with determination, can be overcome

Procrastination, the old saying goes, is the thief of time, and it's something of which we are all guilty. It's also been described as "The Art of Keeping Up with Yesterday."

We venture into the spare room to look for something we stowed away months ago and say to ourselves, "I'll have to clean this mess up soon." Then we shut the door, literally and symbolically, hiding it from our eyes. We may even resolve to tackle it the next day, but of course, then there will be another excuse. Procrastination never lets up. The friend of laziness, it promotes guilt and a feeling of resentment at our own weakness.

Having an untidy spare room may seem trivial in the scheme of things, but it's symbolic of the problems procrastination can bring, especially in our approach to work. Whatever we do for a living, there is always a multitude of tasks, some more challenging than others that need to be tackled. Putting off until another time what can, and should be done right away, can also create a multitude of troubles. We all know that today's minor task left undone becomes tomorrow's major problem. The report that should be finished today, those appointments that must be made for the visiting executives.

So why do we procrastinate? Is it just laziness, a kind of torpor that we find difficult to shake off? Or is it simply a lack of motivation? If, for example, we knew that important guests were on their way to stay with us, that spare room would doubtless be cleaned up in no time. And if we knew that by completing our tasks at work in a timely fashion we would be in line for an important promotion, wouldn't we then redouble our efforts to catch up with all our outstanding tasks, even doing some things ahead of time?

For many of us, our student days shape our attitudes to life. These are times when procrastination rules or is seen as a challenge to be overcome. In my case, I had been studying hard for weeks, burning the midnight oil, doing my best as I thought, to prepare myself for the upcoming exams. Some nights I would simply fall asleep with a book in my hands and wake up the next morning still dressed in yesterday's clothes. After a shower, a snacked breakfast from the fridge, and a change of clothes, I would resume my cycle of reading, researching, eating, and occasionally falling asleep.

From time to time, I would gaze around my apartment which had deteriorated into an untidy mess and resolve yet again to do something about it "as soon as I have time." Finally, one bleary-eyed evening I ran out of food and had to venture out to the 24-hour supermarket around the corner. As well as food and essentials, I had the foresight to buy a pack of large black garbage bags, thinking to myself that they would come in useful later.

Laden with my shopping, I was struggling to get the key into the door of my small apartment when I noticed a strange and unpleasant odor. By the time I had managed to juggle the bags of shopping and open the door I realized much to my embarrassment, that the smell was coming from my own kitchen. The overflowing waste bin, the dishes crammed into the sink, the pile of unwashed laundry . . . procrastination had caught up with me in a big way—and I liked it not one bit.

Not liking it is one thing, but doing something about it, especially at that hour when all I wanted to do was to fill my stomach and sleep, was a challenge I thought I was about to fail. I had found a place to deposit the shopping and looked around, assessing what I would have to do in the Big Cleanup. Tomorrow, it will have to be tomorrow I thought, feeling I simply had no energy to tackle it there and then. Procrastination looked like it was about to steal another chunk out of my life. Just then though, I made a great decision. Before I go to bed, I said to myself, I will do all the dishes, clean the fridge and put the shopping away. At least I will have made a start; the rest of the cleaning I would do the next day.

Yes, you've guessed what happened. Once I had got into the swing of things I simply carried on until the Big Cleanup became Mission Completed. I even found a text-book I had been convinced must have self-destructed but which reappeared in the laundry basket; living in an untidy mess can result in some strange things.

My big lesson from that early encounter with my own procrastination was, that like so many of life's problems, once tackled head-on and with determination, it can be overcome. And the rewards are many. There is of course the immediate and practical benefit of simply getting the job done. There's the sense of satisfaction of having risen successfully to the challenge. There's also a new clarity of mind, free from the nagging distractions of things yet to be done, a clarity that inspires you to stay ahead of the procrastination game.

In my case, working in a clean and orderly environment made my studying so much easier. I planned my schedule, including time out for exercise and relaxation and daily chores around the apartment. This meant cleaning up after every meal, doing the laundry on a regular basis, not staying up too late, and getting up early.

Most of the jobs we put off doing, tend to be those we regard as unpleasant and time consuming. We know they have to be done, but we relieve our guilt by doing the easy and fun jobs first. To escape from the relentless pressure of procrastination we must approach every task in a mindful and humble fashion, aware of the moment.

Whether tending to our daily chores, checking and replying to our e-mail, getting that report done on time, everything we do deserves our full attention. When we provide that, the completion of each task will have its own reward.

Naturally, not everything can be given top priority, but by applying a planned and systematic approach to the jobs that will always lie ahead, we will banish procrastination from our lives and become skilled practitioners of that other art—"The Art of Keeping Up with Tomorrow."

Empty words

Don't make promises if you can't keep them

"OK, I promise I'll have it done by the weekend." Are you sure?" "Yes, I'm sure—don't worry, I promise." Making promises is something we all do. More often than not, we also break them. Children quickly learn the value of those two words, "I promise." They seem to offer a perfect way to turn off the flow of parental nagging. "Please, Mom, all my friends are going. I won't be on my own. You don't have to worry, I promise I'll come straight home as soon as the concert's over."

In turn, parents will use the promise to control their children. "OK, you two, I need you to be on your best behavior when our visitors arrive. If you show what really good children you can be, then I promise there'll be a trip to the beach on the weekend. Plus I promise to ask your father for that raise in allowance."

We make promises to others and to ourselves. "I've always promised myself that one day I'll take a trip to Europe . . ." Often those kinds of promises remain unfulfilled, but they serve to spur us on. To work harder at whatever we're doing so that one day we'll be free to pursue our dreams. We tell ourselves that everyone needs a dream, remembering perhaps the words of that song from the musical *South Pacific*:

"You gotta have a dream,
If you don't have a dream.
How you gonna make your dream come true?"

Daydreams, vague ambitions that one day we'll make our mark, earn the respect of others, especially that of our peers, by some great achievement so we can bask in the glory of recognition, these surely are harmless promises to ourselves. Don't they help us cope with the business of getting through another day? After all, we say, for some people, dreams do come true.

We often hear of individuals who have achieved a long-held ambition and who seem to revel in what they're doing. "This is something I've always wanted to do. I feel

I'm the luckiest person alive. I love my work, and I'm actually getting paid for it," they say.

But realizing those dreams, making those self-promises come true, demands a little more than just wishful thinking. Yes, we need to think out a strategy, we must have a plan, but if we are to succeed it must be a plan of action. Along the way we can dream a little, look ahead to when we too can say, "This is what I've always wanted to do." But we have to make it happen.

A cynical view of promises is that they are the stock-in-trade of politicians and the currency of people who owe us money. In fact a promise to pay is the very foundation of trade and commerce. There is, for example, the Promissory Note—a document that promises to pay a given sum to a stated payee on a certain date. In some cultures, promises are undertaken on behalf of others, and sometimes, no doubt, against their will. A young woman is promised as a bride by her parents; she in turn may have to promise to do their bidding to keep them free of debt.

Less cynically, young romantics will pledge their undying love, promising to remain ever faithful to one another. In fiction at least, dying heroes extract promises from those comforting them. "Promise you'll take care of my young Beth, promise me now."

More cynics will say that promises are made to be broken—mere devices to buy time, to win someone's favor, to tempt them with that promise of a lifetime, an offer too good to refuse. The implication being, of course, that people foolish or gullible enough to believe such empty promises, deserve what they get, or rather don't get.

The very notion of being promised something extravagant by others can cause us to be instantly suspicious of their motives. Why are they promising so much? Can they really make good on their promises? All this doubt and suspicion raised by a simple expression intended to reaffirm our sincerity, our intention to do what we've said we will do.

The cynicism associated with the promise has given rise to several shrewd observations, including an old Arab proverb stating that a promise is a cloud; fulfillment is rain. Napoleon Bonaparte advised that the best way to keep one's word is not to give it, and George Chapman, an early English writer, observed that a promise is most given when the least is said.

One area where not keeping promises can have devastating effects is at work. And the conventional wisdom here is: don't. Don't make them if you can't keep them. Breaking promises of meeting deadlines, fulfilling given tasks, even answering e-mails and returning telephone calls—"I'll call you back within 30 minutes,"—can quickly lead to loss of credibility and the trust of colleagues, and perhaps even worse, of employers.

Sometimes, we use the promise as a means of self-discipline. We promise to complete a particular task by a certain time, and by making that commitment to others we give ourselves a self-imposed deadline. This seems to be a sensible way to make sure we get things done on time while also encouraging us not to be lazy.

But why do we need to promise? Why can't we simply do what we say? Isn't it better for us to behave in such a way that people don't need to extract promises from us? In other words, that we do, and not promise, rather than promise and not do.

When we think about it, those two words, "I promise," will be completely unnecessary when we simply follow the basic Dharma wisdom of applying Right Thinking, Right Speaking, and Right Action.

A life of non-stop surprises

Keeping a firm grip on the present is
essential if we are truly to accept our place
in time

At whatever age we are, we are always young or old relatively speaking. A toddler of three or four years old will refer to his year-old sibling as his "baby sister." His seven-year old brother will be his "big brother" and to the eleven-year old, they're his "kid brother and sister." Mom and Dad will talk of them as being their "kids" or perhaps, less derogatorily, their children.

As we progress through life this ingrained habit of thinking of others as being either younger or older than ourselves persists. School friends, colleagues at work, family members and friends, social acquaintances, even public figures and entertainment personalities—they all have their place in our mental age-related filing system.

We also use this method to create a sort of moving private universe where everybody and everything with which they are associated are all relative in the sense of the time and space they occupy, both to one another and to ourselves. As we get older, this leads to us developing a sort of Peter Pan view of the world. Our favorite nephew will always be that fresh-faced youngster who seemed to be permanently attached to a skateboard, and our best-loved singer will be equally ageless in our private and timeless world. This skewed scheme of things can lead to more than a few surprises, even shock.

Just recently, I heard the sound of what today probably qualifies as a "Golden Oldie" from the television in another room. It was one of my favorites, and one I always associated with the American singer Andy Williams—by the way, I'm not that old! There he was in what looked liked a modern production—one of those music videos. He was seemingly waltzing with a lithe, young, and very contemporary beauty. Wow, I thought. He hasn't aged a bit. What's his secret?

Then the scene changed. There was the same young woman and that unforgettable voice of Andy Williams, but this time it seemed to be coming from a white-haired grandfather. I stared unbelieving; surely that couldn't be . . . but those features, although now crowned by thinning white hair, were unmistakable. It was indeed that veteran vocalist, Andy Williams himself. I was shocked, so shocked in fact that I hurried back to my study to look him up. According to the entry in my Book of Favorite Songsters, he was born in 1930! Good old Andy, and silly old me.

The "silly old me" syndrome can give us all sorts of surprises. We watch with amazement for instance at the grasp of computer and IT skills demonstrated by some of today's even very young children.

Not long ago I witnessed a father struggling to do something apparently challenging with his mobile phone. I was close enough to hear his sighs of exasperation. Finally, his son, who looked no more than six or seven years old said, "Give it to me Dad." Within seconds and with one hand still holding a half-licked ice cream he had done whatever was necessary and handed the phone back to his father. Perhaps the father of this pint-sized prodigy was no longer surprised, but I was.

I was so taken aback by the episode that I recounted it later to friends over dinner. Another surprise—none of them was impressed. In fact, they showered me with similar stories of their own. I was humbled and they were surprised by my apparent unawareness of what they said is the reality of our times. I kept quiet for the rest of the evening but I must admit I now view even the very young generation with a new-found respect!

Because we're all guilty of the self-deception that comes from our apparent need to keep the past alive, we must be aware of its dangers. But surely it's harmless enough we say. Isn't it better for example to remember a loved one or even a favorite singer when they were at their best? Fond memories are one thing but a craving for a world and a time, which no longer exists, is both foolish and eventually unrewarding.

Keeping a firm grip on the present is essential if we are truly to accept our place in time. That place, however much we wish we could turn back the pages in the Book of Life, will always be now—the present moment.

We must remind ourselves also that the present is possible only because of the certainty of change in the world as we know it. Fully accepting that truth, will us help us achieve Dharma wisdom and the understanding it brings with it. It's a clarity that comes from breathing, thinking, seeing, speaking, acting—and literally being in and of, the present moment.

DHARMA MOMENTS IN DAILY LIFE

Do not dwell in the past, says the Buddha, do not dream of the future, concentrate the mind on the present moment.

Another veteran performer, Hollywood actor Kirk Douglas, seems to be living in the moment and enjoying it. Not that long ago he agreed to play the grandfather figure in a serialized drama in which most of the actors are members of the Douglas family.

One thing seems for sure—he's likely to hold the attention of the audience whenever his character speaks. Now in his eighties, and recovering from a stroke, which had left him temporarily speechless, he explained that because he has to enunciate very slowly and deliberately he always gets everyone's attention. "They think I am about to say something important," he says—very slowly and deliberately. He also says he's still learning.

That surely, is a lesson for all of us.

The infinite dimensions of the human brain

The brain is an organ that is designed to
change in response to experience

There are two quotes about the
brain that I like. One is the well-known remark by Robert
Frost, "The brain is a wonderful organ. It starts working
the moment you get up and does not stop until you get
into the office." The other is by an unknown author who
no doubt was inspired by the original. "The human brain
is a wonderful organ. It starts working the moment we
are born and stops only when we are about to make our
first public speech." I suppose this kind of plagiarism is
excusable because it rings true. It's also mildly amusing.

Woody Allen has famously said that his brain is his
second favorite organ. What he did not say is that without

a functioning brain he would not be able to enjoy the capabilities of his first favorite. The human brain is indeed a wonderful organ and its amazing capabilities are still being explored with yet more new discoveries confounding long-held scientific ideas.

The brain is an organ that is designed to change in response to experience. Neuroscience and psychological research over the past decade on this topic has burgeoned and is leading to new insights about the many ways in which the brain changes in response to experience.

This basic issue is being studied at many different levels, in different species, and on different time scales. Yet all of the work invariably leads to the conclusion that the brain is not static but rather is dynamically changing and undergoes such changes throughout its entire life.

This flexibility of the brain that allows it to adapt to the ever changing variety of challenges that we constantly throw at it is referred to by the cognitive neuroscientists as "neuroplasticity," a neat and concise term that should require no further explanation, but which in fact describes highly complex processes that change constantly. Those neuroscientists will tell us by the way that this synaptic plasticity forms the basis for adaptation within the brain's neuronal networks.

"Synaptic plasticity" "neuronal networks,"' are of course wonderful conversation stoppers. "It's all a question of synaptic plasticity, and how this makes possible the amazing adaptation that takes places within the neuronal networks."

In other words, the brain is indeed a wonderful organ that works continuously throughout our life. It is also highly adaptable and changes all the time.

What do we mean when we say it changes all the time? According to most neuroscientists, it means that the brain is constantly changing in its physical form and the way it organizes itself.

Those same scientists have made many discoveries recently about how the brain works and how it develops. They point out that at birth, the brain is very immature. In fact, the human brain is not fully mature until at least twenty years after birth. And, during this long development the human brain is highly dependent on, and is modified and shaped by experience. For example, in people born blind, the parts of the brain that normally process visual information are rewired and come to process sounds, including language. In those born deaf, the areas of the brain that normally process sounds come to process vision. In this sense, those individuals "see" with their ears.

The language-relevant brain systems are also shaped by experience. In people who learn a language later than six years of age, the brain systems that normally process grammar are not used. However, the systems that process the meanings of words are normal in late language learners. Children whose parents or teachers talk to them regularly display good language skills and well-organized language brain systems. However children who are rarely spoken to have stunted language development and immature language systems.

Typical human and animal environments are complex and provide a variety of stimuli, and research has shown that such stimulating environments lead to enhanced brain growth, learning and intelligence.

Interestingly, studies of animals and humans demonstrate that nurturing caregivers and low levels of stress are important in producing appropriate levels of the brain chemicals that are necessary for healthy emotional control. High levels of stress and the absence of nurturing caregivers result in high levels of the chemicals that are harmful to these systems.

when we show loving kindness to others it has a real and positive effect on their brain?

So, contrary to what many people used to think, the human brain is a constantly changing, highly dynamic organ—perhaps we can say it's neuroplastic.

All this talk of neuroplasticity may seem a little too technical but it's a fair bet that many of us familiar with *Vipassana* meditation will already be saying to ourselves that we may not be familiar with the scientific terminology, but that we have long understood that our brain is much more than neural pathways and complicated circuitry. And we are well aware of its ever changing nature.

This perhaps inevitable link between Buddhist meditation and neuroscience has recently become even more meaningful as highlighted by a report of the 12th Conference on Mind and Life—an ongoing dialogue between scientists and Buddhist scholars.

The topic of this conference in the presence of the Dalai Lama was none other than neuroplasticity or more fully—Neuroplasticity: The Neuronal Substrates of Learning and Transformation.

The Dalai Lama has long been encouraging Buddhist practitioners to blend their spiritual knowledge with modern scientific knowledge. The Mind and Life Institute says, "Along with his vigorous interest in learning about the newest developments in science, His Holiness brings to bear both a voice for the humanistic implications of the findings, and a high degree of intuitive methodological sophistication.

And His Holiness believes that science and Buddhism share a common objective: to serve humanity and create a better understanding of the world. He feels that science offers powerful tools for understanding the interconnectedness of all life, and that such understanding provides an essential rationale for ethical behavior and the protection of the environment."

At the conference, with the encouragement of the Dalai Lama, neuroscientist Richard Davidson of the University of Wisconsin, scanned the brains of Buddhist monks. The brain activity in volunteers who were novice meditators was compared with that of Buddhist monks who had spent more than 10,000 hours in meditation.

The task was to practice "compassion" meditation, generating a feeling of loving kindness toward all beings.

"We tried to generate a mental state in which compassion permeates the whole mind with no other thoughts," says Matthieu Ricard, a Buddhist monk at Shechen Monastery in Katmandu, Nepal.

In yet another scientific confirmation of the power of meditation, the results of the scans of the monks demonstrated dramatic increase in high-frequency brain activity called gamma waves during compassion meditation. Gamma waves underlie higher mental activity such as consciousness. The novice meditators "showed a slight increase in gamma activity, but most monks showed extremely large increases of a sort that has never been reported before in the neuroscience literature," said Prof. Davidson.

This scientific validation of the yet to be realized power of meditation, is naturally welcome news for all practitioners of *Vipassana* meditation. For most of us, it is also no surprise.

ABOUT THE AUTHOR

Danai Chanchaochai holds a master's degree in marketing (First Class Honors) from Thammasat University and Gothenberg University, Sweden, and a BBA (Gold Medal) from Assumption University. He graduated from Clayton High School, St. Louis, Missouri, as an AFS exchange student.

At present, he serves on the Board of Directors of the Millenium World Peace Foundation (MWPF); Executive Committee of Public Relations department, Thai Rice Foundation under Royal Patronage; Committee of the Classical Music Foundation under the Royal Patronage of HRH Princess Galyani Vadhana Krom Luang Naradhiwas Rajanagarindra; and the Executive Committee of Advertising Association of Thailand for the year 2004–2006. Prior to this engagement, Danai served on the Executive Committee of the Marketing Association of Thailand (MAT), as Managing Director at MDK Consultants (Thailand), as the public affairs manager at American Express (Thai) and as assistant country manager for Thomas Cook Travellers Cheques.

Danai has also served as the Managing Director of DMG Books and he is the founder of Thailand Rights Center, an organization aimed at promoting Thai and Asian literary works to the world. In 2004, he received Priew Awards as one of the top ten role models of Thailand and has been recently listed among Top 500 Society's Prime Numbers (The Essential Guide to the Social Season 2005) by Thailand Tatler, together with 100 Young Executives 2005 by *The Nation Newspaper*.

Danai is also a columnist for several leading publications in Thailand, including *Bangkok Post*, *Krungthep Turakij*, *Manager Daily*, *Business Thai*, *Kom Chad Luek*, and *Praew Magazine* and hosts radio shows under the topics of management and self-development through Buddhism. In addition, he is a well-known editor/translator for several best selling titles including *Asian Branding*, *The Entrepreneur*, *The Big Mango*, *Rebuilding the Corporate Genome*, and *Lateral Marketing*, to name just a few.

He is a guest speaker on topics such as Marketing, PR Strategies, crisis communications, and related issues at various academic and business institutes, including The Asia Business Forum, the Graduate School of Business Administration, Assumption University, and the UN.